Bandits

&Bibles

Convict Literature in
Nineteenth-Century America

Edited by
Dr. Larry E. Sullivan

Akashic Books
New York

Published by Akashic Books
©2003 Larry E. Sullivan

Digital Imaging by Rich Waltman

ISBN: 1-888451-37-8
Library of Congress Control Number: 2002116771
All rights reserved
First printing

Printed in Canada

Akashic Books
PO Box 1456
New York, NY 10009
Akashic7@aol.com
www.akashicbooks.com

For Marie

TABLE OF CONTENTS

Introduction
BY LARRY E. SULLIVAN

Part One
BANDITS, OUTLAWS, AND ROGUES

Part Two
CONVICTS ON CONVICTS

Part Three
LIFE BEHIND THE BARS

Part Four
BIBLES AND REFORM

Introduction

By Dr. Larry E. Sullivan

DURING THE LAST QUARTER of the twentieth century and the turn of the twenty-first, Americans have waged an ongoing battle with the prison system. Beginning in the 1970s, the criminal justice system began turning its back on the concept of offender rehabilitation, with lawmakers determining that true reform wasn't feasible in prison and that taxpayer dollars were going to waste on programs for the incarcerated. Convicts were supposedly being coddled, what with weight-lifting regimes, education programs, television, well-stocked libraries, and other amenities. In their stead, we began instituting a harsher regime with longer sentences for both violent and nonviolent crimes; "no frills" imprisonment; abolishment of parole; more punitive probationary restrictions; and in many criminal justice decisions, both at the trial and sentencing stages, the gradual replacement of the victim as focus instead of the state as surrogate for the victim. These measures began to tilt the balance decidedly against the offender. Legislatures, upset over what they saw as pro-criminal discretionary sentencing on the part of the judiciary, began instituting mandatory sentencing guidelines in the 1980s and abolishing the indeterminate sentence, a hallmark of the Progressive era's prison-reform movement. As the politicians sought to objectify sentences, victim impact statements brought a deep and disturbing subjective element into the process. It is difficult for a criminal to overcome the sympathy a jury and judge give to the victim of a violent crime.

Introduction

This late-twentieth-century backlash took place against a very short-lived movement of prison reform. From the beginning of the penitentiary in the United States in the late eighteenth century, the judicial system basically ignored what went on in our prisons. Prisons were for punishment and judges reasoned that interfering in prison routines would undermine discipline and cause hazardous conditions for staff and convicts alike. Under this hands-off policy, prison officials were allowed to run their institutions as they wished. It was only in 1910 that the Supreme Court, in the case *Weems v. United States,* applied the "evolving standards of decency" test to the treatment of prisoners under the concept of cruel and unusual punishment, as set forth in the Eighth Amendment to the Constitution. But the courts did little else for prisoners' rights throughout most of the first half of the twentieth century.

For many of us, our modern memory of prison conditions goes back only as far as the decisions of the Supreme Court of the Warren era in the 1960s. This period was a time of great social change for America. The civil rights movement, the Vietnam War, and other social movements politicized prisoners and brought the concepts of equal justice and human rights home to the general populace. The courts applied such principles to the lowest element of our society, the criminal. Offender rights, delineated in such court cases as *Gideon v. Wainwright* (1963), *Miranda v. Arizona* (1966), and others, applied due process and equal protection clauses of the Constitution to defendants. And it was only in 1962 in the *Robinson v. California* decision that the Supreme Court brought the states within the purview of the Eighth Amendment. Other decisions, such as *Cooper v. Pate* in 1964, allowed prisoners to sue state officials in federal court for the first time. Such victories ushered in a swarm of prisoners' suits in the 1970s. Convicts won the right to unimpeded access to the courts. Prisons were forbidden to punish convicts who sued or criticized prison administrations. As a result, many critics complained of a stream of never-ending frivolous lawsuits.

The confluence of forces of prisoner rights and prison officials' resentment set the stage for a bevy of prison riots in the 1970s, the most famous being the fatal Attica riot of 1971 and the bloody New Mexico riot of 1980. These riots in turn ushered in a flurry of Supreme Court activity that began chipping away at prisoners' rights. The 1976 case, *Estelle v. Gamble,* stated that the inhumanity of prison conditions was not sufficient to establish cruel and unusual punishment. Prison officials must act with "deliberate indifference" to be judged under the Eighth Amendment. *Rhodes v. Chapman* in 1987 stated that the prison committed a violation only when the convict was deprived of minimal civilized measures of life's necessities. Inconvenience and discomfort of prisoners are not constitutional violations, but are part of the penalty that prisoners pay for their offenses. Other cases during the 1990s upheld this view.

Congress got into the act with such legislation as the Violent Crime Control Act of 1994, which eliminated tax-supported college programs in prisons, and the Prison Litigation and Reform Act of 1996, which severely restricted convicts' access to the courts. What these court and Congressional actions of the 1980s and 1990s did was reaffirm Jeremy Bentham's principle of "less eligibility" for prisoners. Bentham, in his *Principles of Morals and Legislation* (1780), said that the "ordinary condition of a convict ought not to be made more eligible than that of the poorest class of subjects who work for an honest living." That is, a convict should not enjoy a standard of living that is better than the poorest honest people in society. What has happened is that we have attempted a reversion to a late-eighteenth-century tenet regarding criminals. That is why this brief account of the American prison is important in understanding the literature produced in these institutions. It is difficult for us to grasp the conditions that existed before 1910 without an appreciation of prison life under the "less eligibility" principle.

Given the civilizing process that society has gone through with its "evolving standards of decency," as the Supreme Court enunciated in *Weems v. United States* (1910), it is not possible of course to actually return to the time that prisons first developed in the Western world. But the fact that the concept of "less eligibility" has come back into play in sentencing decisions, combined with the harsh conditions of daily life in prison, helps us contextualize nineteenth-century convict literature as opposed to the writing of twentieth- and twenty-first-century prisoners. Much prison literature of the twentieth century was written in a political context that didn't exist in nineteenth-century perceptual modes. The politicization of prisoners, the black pride movement, the anti-war movement, and other similar events gave the literature a much more overtly political turn. To be sure, there is no shortage of literature of confinement that does not evoke a class undertone. And much of this contemporary literature and the stories of modern prisoners are drug-related or take the posture of the gangster. The prevalence of drug-related crime and the harsh sentences meted out for mere possession of drugs in the late twentieth century added a whole new dimension to prison life, and by extension to prisoners' writings. We must remember that most hard drugs were not criminalized until 1914 in the Harrison Narcotics Act, and marijuana was made illegal only in 1937 through the moral entrepreneurship of the Federal Narcotics Bureau and other self-appointed protectors of society. With great numbers of people convicted for narcotic-related offenses, it is no wonder that so much of our modern prison literature centers on drugs. Nineteenth-century convicts used drugs both in and out of prison, and we will read some of their stories. Activities related to drug and alcohol addiction may have landed them in prison, but they were not sentenced because of their addictions.

The prison of the nineteenth century, then, was very different from that of today, and thus the mental context of the convict was light years away from that of today. The nineteenth-century prison was a place of dread and terror. The idea of any amenities in a prison would be totally foreign to both prisoners and prison officials alike. A decent meal and perhaps an interesting book to read would be considered luxurious. The prison was a place designed to remind the convict of the wages of sin. Prison architecture itself embodied the moral terrorism of the nineteenth century. In 1826, an English encyclopedia article on prisons summed up well the idea of the nineteenth-century philosophy concerning prisoners:

> The style of architecture of a prison is a matter of no slight importance. It offers an effectual point of abhorrence. Persons, in general, refer their horror of a prison to an instinctive feeling rather than to any accurate knowledge of the privation or inflictions endured. And whoever remarks the forcible operations of such antipathies in the vulgar will not neglect any means however minute of directing them to a good purpose. The exterior of a prison should, therefore, be formed in the heavy sombre style, which most forcibly impresses the spectator with gloom and terror.

Most American prisons in the nineteenth century were built in this style, intended to convey the horrors of imprisonment. Such leftovers of nineteenth-century prison architecture as the old Maryland Penitentiary in downtown Baltimore illustrate the feeling of despair and gloom upon first encountering the "big house." Life in prison was difficult. Programs were usually restricted to hard labor. Prisons always emphasized religion, usually of the Protestant variety of hellfire and brimstone, to remind the convicts of their sins against society. What instances of pleasure the prisoners found were few.

* * *

The constant of all prison life is confinement or lack of freedom. Convicts of all centuries experience this life in a cage. And it is that experience that the free world does not entirely understand. We all have our strategies of survival. But in prison, locked in small cells, surrounded by violent predators, *daily* survival becomes more pressing. And there is the constant degradation and boredom of the everyday carceral existence. Convicts must devise conscious strategies for psychological survival. Some join gangs, others read, write, or become religious. An outlet common to the prison experience and a theme running throughout convict literature is sex, where one can express some humanity and even emotional feelings. When people are kept in close quarters and have no other release for sexual urges, same-sex activity becomes the norm. Much sex is consensual, but violent rape also exists. The latter is part of the convict game. But some of the imprisoned do form sincere emotional attachments. Such accounts of sexual activity figure very prominently in the genre. In the nineteenth century, often we must look for code words and allusions to sex, but it always exists as a strong undercurrent of men and women in cages. For instance, Walter Wilson in *Hell in Nebraska* writes: "The prostitution that exists is that which is practised by men among men or by men to boys. To make it any plainer would perhaps land me in the federal prison for many years, for it is unfit to print and transmit through the mails." Twenty-first-century standards allow the writer to be much more explicit without worrying about laws. These earlier convicts are more comfortable (and legally safer) writing about the redeeming qualities of religious conversion or finding the philosophical meaning to life.

Most prison stories are not written down on paper. Prison culture is primarily an oral one. Experience passes from mouth to mouth, and it is only the privileged, literate prisoner who is able to document prison tales and lore, and to fashion what is primarily a collective experience to his own situation. The convict-author seeks to live in letters and escape from the obscurity to which the law has condemned him or her. Almost all convict writers are concerned with producing an autobiographical narrative. The great prison writers, most of whom were incarcerated for political or religious reasons, transcended their circumstances and have entered into the literary canon. They were writers and intellectuals before imprisonment. Such writers as Boethius, who penned *The Consolation of Philosophy* while awaiting execution under Theordoric the Ostrogoth in the sixth century; John Bunyan, who wrote his autobiography *Grace Abounding to the Chief of Sinners* while in jail in the seventeenth century; Antonio Gramsci, who developed his Marxist theory of hegemony while imprisoned for a number of years in Italy under the Fascist regime; or the Russian Alexander Solzhenitsyn, who wrote about the Gulag Archipelago while a political prisoner, were already authors before their prison experience.

Unlike the great writers cited above, the literature of the majority of convicts began with their prison experience. Technically the prison experience itself forms prisoner literature; it comes out of a life of confinement and punishment, and is usually written by literate felons who feel a need to pass the time or to express themselves. These are "common criminals" and the vast majority of convicts fit into this category: those who found themselves in prison because of murder, robbery, burglary, rape, and other felonious crimes. Since their books are outgrowths of their prison experience, an experience that to them is singular and often the product of culture shock, these convicts usually author only one book, of a quality that condemns it to one printing and quick public oblivion. But some convict or felon writers are exceptional and have entered into the canon. Most notable is one of the earliest, the fifteenth-century Frenchman, robber, and vagabond, François Villon, who wrote some of the most striking poetry of the late Middle Ages and who escaped the executioner more than once because of the quality of mercy of the Medieval criminal justice system. But convict literature in this book is defined as writings by those convicted of felonies, not political crimes, and whose writing abilities began or were nurtured in prison.

The prisoner-author usually writes about violence because violence or its threat is the common thread of the convict's experience. The convict-author is almost always the hero of his books, and his story is a search for personal fame and salvation. The prisoner attempts to transcend the violence of everyday life through the reassertion of his humanity and the search for a saving grace. Given the collective experience of prison life and culture since the inception of the penitentiary in the late eighteenth century, most prison tales take on similar characteristics and we see a few distinctive genres emerge.

Introduction

From the earliest American prison writings to the present, nonfiction by convicts has, with a few exceptions, been more convincing, exciting, and informative than fiction. Few convict writers could match in fiction the realities of prison existence. In fact, many of the convict memoirs, especially the earlier ones, are far more realistic than regular American fiction. The earliest convict narrative is almost purely confessional. The author offers up experiential moral homilies that are meant to educate the reader. Numerous convicts became religious in prison and hence salvation is found in the next world, not the present. Religion can be a great comfort in prison and the very word *penitentiary* has the religious connotations of penance. This is the *conversion narrative* genre and it is present throughout prison history. Some striking examples that appear in this volume include: *Twice Born; Or, the Two Lives of Henry O. Wills, Evangelist* (1890) and Jerry McCauley's *Transformed; or, The History of a River Thief* (1876). We must note that McCauley began a mission in New York City that is still operating and providing assistance to the homeless and needy.

Although many conversion accounts were sincere, numerous were pious only in convention and were used to describe the deeds of the rogue and rascal in order to entertain. This picaresque tradition has a long history in Western literature, dating from the Spanish novel *Lazarillo de Tormes* (1554). In the picaresque, the author realistically recounts his illegal activities. Ostensibly, the narrator confesses his crime in order to teach a moral lesson. But the main interest lies in the telling of the criminal's thrilling and exciting adventures. Most of the nineteenth-century convict narratives were confessional, and the majority had roguish characteristics. From the earliest American example, *The Memoirs of Stephen Burroughs* (1798), to the present, the narration of a life of rascality was a conventional and popular genre. In fact, the compelling narratives of crimes, arrests and escapes, and life in the nether-world draw us deeply into this literature. Stephen Burroughs recounts the life of the quintessential rogue and rascal as he scams his way through life. Only the names and places have changed in the profession when we read a century later in "From One Who Has Squared It" (*The World of Graft,* 1901) that the protagonist had "begun as what they call a river thief . . . We'd prowl around the wharves, hold up somebody, an' then make a get away in the boat. It was a pretty good graft for young blokes such as we was, an' I made ten times as much dough at night as I did in the daytime in the machine shop." But such crimes can affect the nerves of the criminal. Light-Fingered Jim discusses his antidote in *Autobiography of a Thief:*

> After a gun has grafted for a long time his nervous system becomes affected, for it is certainly an exciting life. He is then very apt to need a stimulant. He is usually addicted to either opium or chloral, morphine, or whiskey . . . I will say one thing for opium, however. The drug never makes a man careless of his burglar appearance [not like whiskey, Jim goes on to explain].

A particularly interesting sub-genre of the picaresque also represented in *Bandits & Bibles* is the outlaw narrative of the nineteenth and early twentieth centuries. Although mainly concerned with bank and train robbing activities and the like, some outlaws wrote about their experiences from behind prison walls. Most notable of these are *The Life of John Wesley Hardin as Written by Himself* (1896), George Sontag's account of his career in robbing trains in *A Pardoned Lifer: Life of George Sontag, Former Member, Notorious Evans-Sontag Gang, Train Robbers* (1901), and Cole Younger's account of the Northfield, Minnesota bank robbery in which he and his two brothers were arrested and incarcerated as Jesse and Frank James made their escape.

Nineteenth-century accounts of prison life bring new dimension to our understanding of American history. The harsh conditions of daily life, the punishments, the sparse meals, gave the convicts very little to live for. Only their own survival strategies kept them alive as human beings. The selections published here give a lively account of these conditions, along with descriptions of slang, habits, and daily life.

Introduction

The reader may notice that female convicts are missing from this book. In the nineteenth century the female criminal did not receive the long prison sentences that the male did, and was usually incarcerated for prostitution and other short-term offenses. In other words, they did not have the time to write lengthy memoirs. Women published very few books, and descriptions of their lives are usually confined to such accounts as John Reynolds's *The Twin Hells: A Thrilling Narrative of Life in the Kansas and Missouri Penitentiaries* (1901). We see the same lacuna for black convicts. Entire literary genres spring from the African-American experience, from slavery through the plantation-like penitentiaries in the South after the Civil War. Black prison song and the ghetto toast, for instance, found their way in the blues and oral narrative. But few blacks wrote down their prison experiences in the nineteenth century and we must see their lives in prison through the eyes of whites. For instance, Julian Hawthorne, in his account of a convict's life in *Confessions of a Convict*, tells of the fate of a poor black convict who "died alone, in intense agony, in the seven-by-four stone vault in which he could not breathe."

Many readers were, and still are, drawn to this literature for the vivid and lively descriptions of prison life the convicts provide. We must remember that prisons were intended as dark and gloomy dungeons that confined the detritus of society. Few scholars wrote ethnographies of prison behavior and many prison officials didn't allow convicts to even read the newspaper, much less write about living conditions. As mentioned earlier, even the courts had a strict "hands-off" policy concerning prisons until the twentieth century. With little to restrain prison officials, it is no wonder that we hear accounts, such as D.B. Smith's from *Two Years in the Slave-Pen of Iowa*, of how a convict

> is handcuffed and the pulley hooked on between the cuffs. There are two blocks on the pulley, one of which is fastened on a horizontal beam some twenty feet above the floor, the

other being loose to run up and down at will. All being ready, the officer whose duty it is to punish now pulls on the rope, and up and down goes the poor convict, like a jumping jack in a spectacular show.

Even such famous illustrations of prison life, like that of Sing Sing, which appeared in *Harper's Weekly* in 1867, did little to hide some of the torture devices such as the iron helmet. So these narratives give a rare glimpse into this nether-world of punishment, with its tortures, its daily routines, the friendships forged among convicts, and the rare instances of humanity shared between keeper and kept. An illuminating example of coping skills is Langdon Moore's description of communicating with his wife and circumventing censors by writing messages under a postage stamp.

A striking feature of this nineteenth-century literature is a lack of excuse and the acceptance of responsibility for criminal behavior. Twentieth-century crime and prison narratives are replete with the language of determinism. This determinism could take the form of environmentalism, social disorder, developmental, or other theories of criminology. Nineteenth-century prisoner-authors, on the other hand, largely take responsibility for their crimes. They pride themselves on their personal autonomy. In this stance, many of them apparently subscribed to Hegel's theory of criminal autonomy in *Philosophy of Right,* in which he said:

> His [the criminal's] action is the action of a rational being and this implies that it is something universal and that by doing it the criminal has laid down a law which he has implicitly recognized in his action and under which in consequence he should be brought as under his right . . . Since that is so, punishment is regarded as containing the criminal's right and hence by being punished he is honoured as a rational being. [T. M. Knox, trans., *Hegel's Philosophy of Right,* 1945]

These convicts were Hegelians without knowing it.

Introduction

Outwardly, most convicts adapt to prison regimentation. To conform is the only way to survive the system and perhaps be released. But conformity is not real behavior-modification; it is only the convict's part in the carceral game. We see in these selections that to the prisoner the culture is inverted, a world turned inside out where the rubric of "thief" or "grifter" is a badge of honor, worn proudly and not with scorn. He even has his own colorful language, with words, according to Prisoner Number 1500, "that are distinctively the possession of the thief and convict, whose use would be applicable to no other condition than his." His is a rebellion against the outside world, and inner freedom is his sole criterion or ethic. In prison, the convict is forced to turn his gaze away from the external and toward himself and his moral autonomy. The greater the attempt to break the convict, the greater the resistance. Since most of the lives recounted in nineteenth-century convict narratives were so alien to a middle-class reader, the authors fed their audience's curiosity of this strange but fascinating world of the underclass criminal. To the reader of the period, these accounts could be sensationalistic, and some of the best written are pointedly so. But most of the authors have a sincere desire to tell their stories and recount how they survived their ordeals.

During the Progressive period of the late nineteenth century, prison reform took on the goal of rehabilitation as well as that of punishment. Sociologists and psychologists set out to reform prisoners in some highly notable, but failed experiments. The prison became a laboratory for the new social sciences. We do not see this type of reformation during the earlier part of the century. Prisoners found their own salvation from within, whether through literature, philosophy, or God. Andrew George, in *The Texas Convict,* states this personal reformation bluntly: "It has been amply demonstrated in the history of crime that a criminal can be reformed, at least some of them. My ideas about reform are short and simple—the reform must start with the man himself." Or take Light-Fingered Jim (*Autobiography of a Thief*), who found solitary confinement liberating—which helped him break his opium habit, after which he went on to discover a literary bent. He recounts:

> For me, prison life had one great advantage. It broke down my health and confirmed me for many years in the opium habit . . . ; but I educated myself while in stir. Previous to going to Sing Sing my education had been almost entirely in the line of graft; but in stir, I read the English classics and became familiar with philosophy . . .

Jim then goes on to describe his reading and delightfully compares some famous literary characters to people he had known on the graft. Is it any wonder that he was taken with a character like Becky Sharp from Thackeray's *Vanity Fair,* who is likened to a clever grafter he once knew?

Many prisoners turned to religion to achieve reformation. Conversion literature is a time-honored literary genre, but is nowhere so striking than when it comes from a prison cell. In the twentieth century, we might only think of Malcolm X, and his journey to religion during his years in the Massachusetts penitentiary, to feel the power of conversion. But most convict narratives in any century do not have the force of Malcolm X's account; still, they do abound in the literature, and many are infused with the same sincerity and religious feeling. As Franklin Carr recounts in *Twenty-Two Years in State Prisons* (1893), after he fell on his knees and prayed for a long time, he "felt as if a heavy burden had rolled off of me and I felt like shouting for joy, for I knew that the Lord had heard my cry for mercy . . ." He then went on to tell "what a wonderful Saviour I have found and speaking to those that were down in the gutter of sin and crime where I myself had been." Or listen to such prison poetry as J. Wess Moore's "The Penitent Convict's Prayer" (1908), where his "Wrongs were cruel and many/ While Satan was leading along/ shame hath hidden my gladness,/ I live with the convict throng."

We end this book in the early twentieth century. A turning point in convict literature came with Donald Lowrie's *My Life*

Introduction

in Prison (1912). This compelling narrative was an early and influ-
ential example of the convict who feels he was driven to crime
because of social and class inequality. Lowrie's book inspired
Thomas Mott Osborne to begin his career as one of the most
well-known prison reformers of the twentieth century. Narratives began to change after Lowrie's book, and elements of class-
driven crime and politicization of prisoners marked much of
twentieth-century prison literature. Autonomy gave way to social, economic, and environmental determinism. And the new
breed of sociologists began studying prisoners *in situ*, bringing
their social-science methods and interviewing techniques into
the world of the prison. Classic works in criminology resulted,
but most did not catch the flavor of the convict-author who
wrote for an audience much different from the academy.

What the sociologists did for convict ethnography in the
twentieth century, these books, with a close reading, do for the
nineteenth century. These are some of the only descriptions
we have of the life of the outlaw, criminal, and convict—from
their point of view. To be sure, many moralist and benevolent
prison reformers existed in the nineteenth century, and we
have their treatises on prison discipline. But these tracts pay
short shrift or demean the ideas or opinions of the common
criminal. Most reformers were not interested in ethnography
but in moral rehabilitation. Therefore, most of what the
academy has written about convict life in this period is skewed
toward the prison official and reformer. Bringing many of
these little known works to light provides insightful glimpses
into the life and mentality of convicts of the nineteenth century, as these writers paint valuable landscapes and portraits
unavailable elsewhere.

* * *

I have retained the grammar, spelling, and punctuation presented
in the original texts for each selection. I have also provided a
short introduction to each of the book's four parts.

* * *

I began collecting convict literature in the 1970s when I worked at the Maryland Penitentiary, a maximum-security institution in Baltimore. My research interests quickly focused on convict memoirs, and over the past twenty-five years I have built up a considerable library of this literature. Most are first editions, because very few of these books went beyond the first printing, much less another edition. In this sense, they are rare, and in this book I have attempted to share with a greater public some of the scarcer items not found in many, if any, research libraries. I have used some of these writings for a variety of publications, including two editions of a history of prison reform in America. Over one hundred of these books were exhibited first at the Grolier Club of New York in 1997–98 and twice at John Jay College of Criminal Justice, in 1998 and 2000. At these institutions I gave talks on the literature of confinement and I am thankful to them both for providing a vehicle for the viewing and further understanding of this literature and the criminal and convict lives the books describe.

I would like to thank my secretary, Nicole Demerin, for the variety of tasks she performed in bringing this project to completion. I owe a special debt of gratitude to my research assistant and student, Kimberly Spanjol, for her close reading of the selections, and her efforts, enthusiasm, and support for this work.

Larry E. Sullivan
New York City
Ascension Thursday, 2002

Part One

BANDITS, OUTLAWS, AND ROGUES

M ANY NINETEENTH-CENTURY READERS turned to convict memoirs for stories of daring robberies, con games, and roguish adventures. We present here a variety of some of the most interesting narratives of outlaw and criminal life in the nineteenth century. Stephen Burroughs, for example, was a self-described thief and rogue. He led a riotous life full of criminal adventure, arrests, jail escapes, and other illegal activity. His is the earliest American convict memoir. Writing in the picaresque tradition, Burroughs here describes his trial for felonious assault on three girls committed when he was a schoolmaster. Simeon Coy was involved in election corruption in Indiana and spent time in that state's penitentiary. In this selection he provides readers with a lively description of crooks and criminals he had known.

The subtitle of Henry Wills's book vividly describes its content: *Remarkable Experiences as a Wharf-rat, a Sneak-thief, a Convict, a Soldier, a Bounty-Jumper, a Fakir* . . . Wills discusses one of his many con schemes. Later on in this book he talks of his escape attempt and resulting punishment. To be sure, John Wesley Hardin was one of the most famous of nineteenth-century American outlaws. An unreconstructed southerner from Texas, he murdered an ex-slave in 1868. He escaped the law and experienced a number of adventures, including a run-in with Wild Bill Hickok over another murder, until the Texas Rangers caught up with him in 1877 and sent him to prison in

Huntsville, Texas. In prison he studied theology and law and was pardoned in 1894. A year later, at the age of forty-two and a practicing attorney, he was gunned down in a saloon in El Paso, Texas. In this selection, he describes his trial for the killing of a deputy sheriff in Comanche, Texas, which landed him in prison.

We can characterize two subsequent entries, those by Josiah Flynt and Hutchins Hapgood, as "assisted biography," a term coined by Hapgood. Flynt, a journalist, spoke with an anonymous criminal to "get him to talk" about "the Under World's criticism of the Upper World's system of municipal defence against crime." His criminal relates a dynamic and fast-paced tale of criminal misadventures in Chicago, Boston, and New York. Hapgood was a noted journalist at the turn of the twentieth century and his first important work, *The Spirit of the Ghetto* (1902), became a journalistic classic in which he used sociological, biographical, and journalistic methods to create a vivid portrait of ghetto life. In *Autobiography of a Thief* he conducted repeated interviews with an habitual criminal. In one of the most compelling narratives of this picaresque genre, Hapgood related Light-Fingered Jim's trials and tribulations as a burglar, his use of opium, his girlfriends, and his narrow escapes from the law.

Two famous outlaws wrote the last two selections in this section. Cole Younger was one of the most daring and noted outlaws of the nineteenth century. After the Civil War, Younger, an ex-Confederate soldier, along with his three brothers—Jim, Bob, and John—teamed up with other ex-Confederates Frank and Jesse James to form the James-Younger Gang, perhaps the most notorious gang of bank and train robbers of the century. But back in their home of Missouri they were heroes and martyrs for a lost cause, especially when John Younger was killed in a gunfight with the hated Pinkerton agents. For a time there was a movement in the Missouri House of Representative to declare amnesty for the gang. The amnesty resolution was narrowly defeated and attempts to revive it were dashed by the attempted robbery of a bank in Northfield, Minnesota on

September 7, 1876. The robbery was foiled when a cashier sounded the alarm. One cashier was killed, another wounded, and Cole Younger took eleven bullets during his daring escape and rescue of his brothers. All three Youngers were eventually captured as they roamed the unfamiliar Minnesota territory, while the James brothers fled successfully. This robbery has been the subject of a number of books and movies. Here Cole Younger describes the action, the gunfire and general melee during and after the robbery, and, briefly, his twenty-five years in the Minnesota State Prison. He was paroled in 1901, pardoned in 1903, and eventually teamed up with Frank James to tour with Buffalo Bill's Wild West Show. He never revealed the names of the two outlaws who escaped the Northfield fiasco, although it was widely known they were the James brothers.

George Sontag was another famous train robber at the end of the nineteenth century. The Sontag-Evans gang held up numerous trains in California during the last part of the nineteenth century. Many of the robberies were blamed on the infamous Dalton gang (Emmett, the lone surviving Dalton after a shoot-out in Coffeyville, Kansas, wrote a memoir in the 1930s), but even after the Daltons left for Missouri and Oklahoma, the robberies continued. Law enforcement officials finally identified George Sontag and Chris Evans as the leaders of the gang that, in the words of *Munsey's Magazine* of February 1902, "had done so much to make travel on California railroads exciting . . ." In the introduction to his memoir, Sontag was identified as having been reared "with all the advantages of a good Christian, homeloving mother . . ." and accuses "no one for his sorrowful life, other than evil associates, and these companions were not sought through necessity . . . He chose to cast his lot with men whose lives had been failures . . ." He was sent to Folsom Prison, "one of the most notoriously known prisons on the coast . . ." where "most cruel and barbarous treatment has been practiced upon the unfortunate inmates . . ." In the selection presented here, Sontag embarks on the criminal life with his first robbery.

Twice Born

By Henry O. Wills

From Twice Born; Or, The Two Lives Of Henry O. Wills, Evangelist (Being a Narrative of Mr. Wills's Remarkable Experiences as a Wharf-Rat, a Sneak-Thief, a Convict, a Soldier, a Bounty-Jumper, a Fakir, a Fireman, a Ward-Heeler, and a Plug-Ugly. Also, a History of His Most Wondrous Conversion to God, and of His Famous Achievements as an Evangelist (Cincinnati: Western Methodist Book Concern, 1890).

I thought I would try Chicago and see if I could not make a fortune there. I have said before that almost anybody can steal, but it takes a smart man to hide; and I say further, any man that has brains, if he sets out to do it, can make money, but it takes a man with more brains to keep it after he has it.

Well, I went to Chicago with the can-opener, and I made money, as I did in the oil regions, and spent it in about the same way as I did there. I believe if I had been like some men I could have been a millionaire to-day; but, suppose I had become one, the question is, Would I know Jesus as I do now know him?

I worked Chicago until it seemed to me that every man, woman, and child in the city had a can-opener, so I had to find something new. This I did, and in handling the new article, I found that Barnum was right when he said that "the American people were the easiest people on earth to be humbugged." I have proved the truth of these words of Barnum in a great many ways. I have sold perfume made of paraffine and oil of wintergreen or bergamot, and done up in tinfoil, which sold for twenty-five cents a package, and only cost five mills; that is, sold for two hundred and fifty mills an article which cost five mills. I sold a non-explosive coal-oil powder, made of colored salt, for twenty-five cents a box. It cost me three mills. I sold the California diamond polish, said to have been made in San Francisco, and good for all things, but in reality made of Akron water-lime. This polish sold for three dollars per dozen, and it could be bought for a dollar and a half per barrel. One of the best sellers I had in Chicago, after the can-opener, was a fan.

Only think of men buying fans in the dead of winter; but they did, and they bought of me. I had almost the first that were made. They were called the Magic Fan (they are very common now). It pulled open from a tube-shaped handle with a cord and tassel; and pulling on the other end would close it again. It would have surprised even Barnum if he could have seen how I sold those fans that winter.

Now, friends, I was working all this time; still I was "crooked," and would steal when the opportunity offered itself; but I was very, very watchful and careful, for I did not want to do any more time, and I never have.

People often wonder how the crooks know where a man carries his money, and how thieves can get into their houses and know where the valuables are kept. Now, suppose you are traveling on the cars, or you are waiting in the depot. The "mob," as it is called, is made up of three or five persons, who travel together. One of these is called the "wire," and it is his business to "go through" you, and get your money. It is done in this way: The "mob" comes into the car or depot, and cries: "Look out for pickpockets!" Any man having money on his person, and not up to the trick, will, on hearing the alarm, put his hand at once over the pocket that holds the cash. Doing this, till that good-looking gentleman, the "wire," who has an eye like a hawk, sees just where to put his hand and get what he wants. Then the "mob," or one member of it, cries out for passengers to take the next car for such and such a place, or "change cars," "all aboard," or something of the kind, and when the people make a rush to get in the right car, the gang will crowd about the door and push, while the nice man just behind you, or the one coming in while you are trying to get out, has taken your money. Suppose you have your hands in your pockets, with your pocketbook in your hands; all the thieves have to do is to push each other and rush you about; then one of them will hit you on the top of the head and drive your hat down over your eyes. Out come your hands to lift your hat so you can see. Your pocket is unguarded, and—biff!—your money is gone, and the crowd also.

So beware of the cry, "Pickpockets!" either in the car or depot. Keep your hands still! Don't tell them where you keep your money. To do this will sometimes require an effort, because most men, knowing where their money is, find that their heart is there also. "For where your treasure is, there will your heart be also" (Luke xii, 34).

I have seen a man who was smart—at least he thought he was—and after a "mob" had "worked" a depot, and eight or ten people had lost their wealth, he was saying, "What fools the traveling public are!" and all such talk. When the conductor came along for tickets, this man would put his hand in his pocket to get the book that held his ticket, only to jump to his feet and shout: "I have been robbed!" Probably the very man he had been giving the talk to about his smartness had gone through him while he was telling it, to pass the pocketbook to his pal in the next seat behind him, and he to another, and so on, until one of them would go with it into the water-closet, where he would skin it. That is, he would take the money out, and drop the book on the track.

In this way thieves do their work, and it is but one of a hundred equally dishonorable schemes.

From One Who Has "Squared It"

BY JOSIAH FLYNT

From *The World of Graft* by Josiah Flynt (New York: McClure, Phillips & Co., 1901), author of *Tramping With Tramps* and *The Powers That Prey*.

Thanks to the kind offices of a common friend, it was possible for me to hear him tell his story, and it let in such a flood of light upon the questions with which my investigation was concerned that I have decided to give it here in full, by way of comment upon what has gone before. As he told it, it seems to me one of the most interesting criticisms of municipal defence against crime as found in the United States that I have been privileged to hear, and my only regret is that I am forbidden to give the critic's name. His statement, however, is reported exactly as he made it, except in a few instances, when, to shield his identity, it was necessary to change certain names.

"I ain't a reformed man, Flynt, an' can't talk like one, but the Cap says you want me to chew the rag about municipal corruption, as you call it, an' I can give you my side of it, if that'll do you any good."

"That's exactly the side that I want; go ahead."

"Then I guess I can't do any better than tell you my own story. I'm a Yorker really. 'Course I've knocked about all over, but York has always been my hang-out, an' I go back there ev'ry now an' then an' make a visit. There's a lot o' young ones sprung up since I used to live there, an' I'd have to look over the place again before I could tell you much about them, but I manage to keep track o' most o' the old fellows. I used to belong to Mother Mandelbaum's push.[1]

"As a kid I was trained to be a machinist, an' it was the learnin' that I got in the machine shop that helped me to break safes. I wasn't a peter-man at the start, though; I got to be that after Leslie and Hope took me up.

"I begun as what they call a river thief. A push o' us kids used to own a rowboat on the East River, an' at night, after work

35

was over, we'd prowl around the wharves, hold up somebody, an' then make a get-away in the boat. It was a pretty good graft for young blokes such as we was, an' I made ten times as much dough at night as I did in the daytime in the machine shop. I was livin' with my old woman at the time, but she never got on to me. She'd 'a' croaked, I guess, if she had. I'm sorry now't I didn't give 'er more money, but she knew 't I was only earnin' five a week, an' she'd got on to me 'f I'd handed 'er any more. We needed more, God knows, but you see how I was fixed. I used to hide the money 't I made at night in a hole 't I bored in one o' my bed-posts.

"After a while the old woman died, an' I cut loose altogether. If she'd lived, p'raps she could 'a' kep' me on the level, but I could never 'a' earned more 'n fifteen a week on the level no-how, an I'd got a taste for luxuries. Understand, don't you? That's what's made me a gun. I wanted a lot o' dough, an' the only way 't I knew how to get it was to steal it. If I'd had an ed-ucation it might 'a' been different, but I never went to school in my life, an' to-day I have to sign my name with an X. That's what keeps me back so now. If I had a trained headpiece on me an' could make good reports, I'd get on; but you can't go to school at fifty-nine an' support a wife, too. I can't anyhow.

"Well, some time after my old woman died, old Hope took notice o' me an' let me into his gang as an outsider. I'd been makin' friends with guns all the while, an' the big guns are al-ways lookin' around for fresh talent. It's just the same as it is in the baseball business. Some manager or captain sees a fellow pitch or catch an' makes up his mind 't he can do somethin' with him. Course Hope didn't set me to crackin' safes, right away, but he tried me on the outside part o' jobs. I had to keep watch outdoors while the big fellows was inside gettin' the coin. A fellow that does that an' pipes off places that are to be touched up is called an outsider.

"For the next twenty years after I got to be an outsider I never got arrested, never did a bit o' time an' must 'a' stole well on toward $75,000. An' when they finally did pinch me, it was the Pinkerton people that did it an' not any municipal copper. Durin' those twenty years it was the crooked municipal copper that kep' me from gettin' sloughed up, an' I'd be on the turf yet 'f I'd only had him to deal with. As a rule, when the city copper ain't a dead one he's a crooked one, an' neither of 'em ever kep' me awake o' nights, 'cause the dead one doesn't know anything, an' the crooked one forgets everything after you've bribed him. See?

"Let me tell you how we used to manage things in New York. If we made a get-away all right an' knew that the police wasn't on to us, course we didn't cough up any coin to 'em; but if there was any trouble about the get-away—if the holler was big—one of us used to go direct to the percentage coppers on the force, tell 'em our tale o' woe, whack up the plunder, an' stop worryin'. That was the system in York twenty-five years ago, an' I know it, 'cause I used to work it myself.

"When Byrnes got to runnin' things, there was a change, but I remember percentage coppers under Byrnes as well as under Walling. Just the same I believe that Byrnes was the wisest, an' takin' him all in all, the best elbow York ever had. I did work in the city after he was inspector, an' he didn't get on to some of it either, but he protected the citizens better than any other man they ever had. While he was at the head the only grafts that ever really flourished, as the papers say, was the Tenderloin, the gamblin' joints, an' the queer,[2] an' those are all grafts that don't hurt the citizens a bit, unless they want to get hurt. It's the fellow from the country that they take in, an' Byrnes never put up a bluff about tryin' to protect the countrymen. He was in the Front Office to look after the people o' York, an' I'm one o' the old York thieves that thinks he did his job as well as it could be done. I'll never forget how I fooled him once. It was after I'd got pretty well up in the business and was known, an' he use to try to make us known fellows report at his office when we came to town. Generally we reported if there was nothin' pressin' to keep us away, an' I guess the system was a good one, but you got to have dead honest people under you to put it through, an' Byrnes wasn't always lucky in gettin' that kind.

"One day I turned up in the city after doin' a job out in the country, an' one o' the percentage coppers recognized me in

Broadway an' tackled me for some dough. I'd never liked the fellow, an' I told him to go to the devil. 'Steal your own money,' I remember I said to him. He thought, you know, 't I'd give him some money to keep quiet about my bein' in town. I ditched him for fair two or three days after, right in the Front Office, too. I'd gone up there to see Byrnes, an' he asked me how long I'd been in town.

"'About a week,' I said.

"'Why didn't you report the day you came in?' he asked me.

"'Didn't so-and-so tell you 't I was in town?' I said. 'I gave him $20 an' asked him to report for me.'

"'Is that on the level?'

"'Sure.'

"'Course I lied, but Byrnes was better short o' that fellow than with him. I haven't kept track o' things in York since Byrnes was let out, but from all I hear I don't believe things are any better 'n they were in his time. You'll find the percentage coppers there to-day just as I did when he was in the Front Office, and where you find them the public gets it in the neck. Course I know that things ain't the way they were when old Marm Mandelbaum used to live in the city, but I understand that the queer an' the Tenderloin an' the cribs are still the big grafts, an' you can take my tip for it that the police of a town are crooked when such grafts are allowed.

"Do you know who it is in York that I like? Dr. Parkhurst. Tell him that, if you ever see him. Tell him that you know an old York thief, who ain't reformed either as regards havin' a change o' heart, as the church people say, who told you that he considers Dr. Parkhurst the wisest man in the city, barrin' nobody on the police force or off it. He is the one man in the berg that you can't fool. I realize better 'n you possibly can what it was that he did when he got Tammany on the run. I've known Tammany ever since I struck the turf; I've been protected by it, an' I've helped protect it; an' I know how strong it was in '94. Now, for one man to overthrow it, as I believe that man Parkhurst did six years ago, is one of the biggest things I know anything about. Mind you, I don't say that 'cause Parkhurst is a preacher, or 'cause I'm stuck on morality. I say it because it was a big stunt, just as holdin' up an express train single-handed is a big stunt. As a gun, I used to like Tammany. Every organization like that makes a town easier for a gun to live in, and if I were on the road to-day an' expected to live in York I'd want Tammany to hold the offices. But, as things are now with me, if the citizens 'ud make Parkhurst chief, an' I could get on the force, I'd work for him on the level—cross my heart, if I wouldn't. He's a whole bunch in himself an' I like him."

He paused for a moment to relight his pipe, and when he spoke again it was in continuation of his own personal story:

"I fell for the first time down South. The tumble hurt pretty bad, 'cause I'd got to think I was never goin' to get caught. Bob Pinkerton copped me out, an' I got a five spot up in Connecticut. I had my choice of a stir³ down South or the one in Connecticut, an' I decided to stand trial for the Connecticut job. It was a jool'ry touch, an' the fellow 't I'd done it with turned state's evidence. I ought to 'a' known better than to pal with him, 'cause he was a second-class gun, but I ditched him proper when I got out. He was doin' fence work in York an' I helped send 'im up the river for eight years. He was the first and last man that wasn't first class that I ever worked with after I got well into the perfesh.

"In '85 I went to England. I made a couple o' pretty good touches, an' then fell hard in Birmingham. It was a jool'ry job again, an' me an' my pal had got into the store all right—it was about seven o'clock in the morning—an' I was standin' near the door peekin' through the letter-box slit an' holdin' the bag for the swag behind me. My pal was fillin' it. Pretty soon a postman came along, an', as luck would have it, he had a letter for the jool'ry store, an' tried to drop it in the slit while my nose was next to it. Course the letter didn't go through, an' the postman kept on pushin' till I got my nose away. We lay low, but the postman had got suspicious, and pretty soon I see two fly-cops go by on the other side o' the street. We tried to make a get-away at the top o' the building, but we found the cops waitin' for us, an' was both caught. We got four years in the same stir that Bidwell was doin' life in for that Bank o' England job. He had it better 'n I did though, 'cause he was in the kitchen where he could get something to eat. I used to be so hungry that I'd pick up the crumbs off the bench after I'd eaten my bread. Those Britishers know how to punish, let me tell you that. If we punished guns in this country the way they do we wouldn't have so many of 'em. I know, 'cause I've done bits in both countries.

"After gettin' out o' the stir I did another job up in Edinburgh, an' came the nearest to gettin' caught without the thing comin' off 't I've ever been in my life. Me an' my pal had shifted to Liverpool after doin' the job, an' as it happened, took a couple o' rooms that two Fenians had just left. We had the swag—mostly diamonds—in our belts, but my pal had left a diamond ring in one of his shoes in the trunk. Two Scotland Yard people knocked at the door one day, an' told us that they wanted to examine our luggage. We didn't know anything about the Fenians havin' been in the rooms, an' was leary as the devil. The coppers found the ring 't my pal had forgotten, an' I thought it was all off.

"'Where'd this come from?' they said.

"'It's mine,' I said; 'I carry it there thinkin' it's safer.'

"They took the con, an' not findin' any revolutionary stuff, made up their minds 't we was all right. We fenced the swag over here.

"In '91 I went back to Europe again, but didn't do much except try to pipe off a jool'ry place in Havre. There's a fellow in London that sends out mobs to do work on the Continent, an' he asked me to take a look at the Havre place. Well, sir, I never had a queerer experience in my life than on that trip. You see, I can't speak anything but English, an' when I got to Havre an' begun pipin' off that jool'ry place I got so leary 'cause I couldn't understand what the people about me was sayin' that I thought they was talkin' about me all the while, an' I'd go miles out o' my way, thinkin' they was pipin' me off."

"Did you go up on the hill to the convent where there's a fine view of the harbor?"

"God only knows where I went. All I know is that I took rides on every street-car they got, tryin' to dodge people 't I was crazy enough to think was watchin' me. In London I wouldn't 'a' been a bit leary, but I'd never been in a place before where I couldn't understand the lingo, an' I got so bughouse 't I never finished my job.

"I was to find out how the jool'ry place was protected an' make a report, but all I was able to tell the boss in London when I got back was that there was no burglar wires. He never asked me to go to France again.

"I came back here in '93, an' made up my mind to try an' square it. I was gettin' old, my way o' openin' was out o' date for the new safes, my dough was all gone, an' I thought I'd better settle down. The only thing 't I could do an' earn any money was bein' a fly-cop, an' I got a job. Things went along pretty well for a couple o' years, an' I was makin' my forty a week when an old pal came to me an' asked me 'f I'd help him open up an old express peter[4] down 'n Louisiana. There was five thousand in it, he said, an' it was easy to break. Course I was a fool to listen to him, but, Flynt, an old thief can no more stand prosperity than he can do time an' not be glad when he's turned loose. I'd been livin' good, you know, havin' reg'lar feed an' the like, an' the old thought about makin' a number one strike an' winnin' out came back to me. I thought if we could get that five thousand we could shift to Australia, where my kind o' business was still rather new then, make a pile, an' then come back here an' live on the level. If my pal hadn't had a girl down in New Orleans 't he wanted to see before we left for Australia, p'raps things 'ud 'a' gone the way I hoped, 'cause we got the five thousand all right an' made a clean get-away. I kep' the dough an' my pal went to New Orleans, but he hadn't been there more 'n a day when he was copped out on suspicion. They put him in the sweat-box,[5] made him cough, an' you know the rest. After I got out o' the stir, all I had to my name was five dollars an' the bummest suit o' clothes 't I've had since I was a kid. I came here, got this job, an' have been here ever since.

"I say 't I ain't reformed, 'cause it's never been a question o' right an' wrong with me. Course I've always known 't ain't on the level to steal, but, as I told you in the beginnin', I wanted a lot o' money an' I went after it the best way I knew how. I've worked harder for the dough 't I've got at different times than people know anything about. You asked me whether there is any fascination, as you call it, about stealin'. Not a bit. I've never been happy till the job I was doin' was over an' the swag or the dough planted. It's all rot about there bein' any fun in crooked work. Why, I've had to leave men inside a bank for thirty-six hours without anything to eat or drink 'cause people was watchin' me. Do you call that fun, an' how do you think I felt while the men was cursin' me for not passin' 'em in their nourishment? There ain't a harder life goin' than that o' the first-class gun, an' all I've got to show for mine is fifty-nine years an' pretty good health. 'Course it don't count for much comin' from one who didn't win out, but I'm here to tell you just the same, after a good long experiment with it, that a criminal life ain't worth what you got to pay for it. It's too swift. There's only one of my old gang that's got any money to-day, an' he's the fellow in London. The rest are all dead or on the hog. Look at Jim Dunlap, who was copped out in Illinois the other day for doin' that bum peter job. He use to be in our mob, an' was recognized as a first-class gun. To-day he's knockin' about breakin' into country stores."

"Why is it that the guns don't save money for old age?"

"They can't do it. When they make a strike the first thing they want to do is to blow themselves, an' that costs money. They want to blow themselves 'cause they never know what day's goin' to be their last. When I'd made a get-away after doin' a job, I was never satisfied till I'd blown in ev'ry dollar. First thing I did was to tog up with the best clothes an' jool'ry 't I could buy. Then I'd go to some town where I wasn't known an' have a good time. When my dough was all gone, I'd tackle another job. Ev'ry gun is the same way. He hits it up hard until the coin gives out; then he goes to work again. If he's pinched before the next touch comes off, he has the satisfaction o' knowin' that he had a good time out o' the last touch anyhow.

He thinks about it all the while he's shut up, an' when he gets out he goes after some more coin to blow himself again.

"There's one thing that lots o' guns do 't I always was shy of, an' I think now that not doin' it helped to keep me from gettin' caught durin' those twenty years. I never let women into my confidence. The average gun goes an' ties up with a woman on the first good touch he makes. The only woman that ever knew much about me while I was graftin' was old Marm Mandelbaum in York, an' she only knew 'cause she was a fence. I like women, mind you, an' am married now, but they tumble more guns 'n all the coppers in existence. The Bidwell boys fell 'cause they told their wives about that Bank o' England touch. They might be alive an' rich to-day if they'd kept their mouths shut. The trouble with guns' wives is that they get a grouch on or get jealous, the only thing they know to do is to go an' squeal on their husbands. A copper can get a lot out of 'em, too, before they know 't he is a copper. They get to chewin' the rag careless like, an' the first thing they know they've told the whole story. A man 't 's on the level don't care, but a gun can't afford to have a wife that's a mouth-piece. If a young fellow that was just startin' out in the business came to me for advice, I'd tell him not to tie up with any woman till he'd made his pile, and never to tell her where his pile came from. I'm sure that that's what helped to keep me under cover so long. Ev'ry now an' then I get to goin' over my recollects an' thinkin' out things, an that's one of 'em. Course there was a lot o' just natural dodgin' an' layin' low, but the two things that helped most was not fallin' in love an knowin' how to touch up the coppers. Since I've squared it I've picked me out a mate; but I could touch up a copper still."

"Do you think the cities are any less corrupt than when you were on the road?"

"From all 't I hear about York, I guess 't a gun can do business there all right yet, but, as I told you, I ain't been back there very recently. Chi is as rotten as it ever was. The place is full o' percentage coppers. I ain't been in Phillie for years, but if it's the way it used to be, a man can make a spring there as well as anywhere else. Bean-Town I never knew much about, but it turns out a lot o' good guns, an' there's generally considerable doin' where they come from. I don't see much change in any o' the towns. The pub's just as ignorant as ever 'bout what goes on, an' the coppers ain't makin' it any wiser.

"I tell you where I have seen changes though — the guns today know more in a minute 'n I did in a week. That's a fact. I could no more get out an' compete with the guns on the turf now 'n I could stand ten years on my head. You wouldn't think it, but it's the truth. This generation o' thieves beats the last one hands down. Course our push there in York had a big name, an' the newspapers still chew the rag about it from time to time, but Leslie, Red Leary, an' all of 'em was greenhorns, let me tell you, compared with the guns workin' now. The pickpockets are swifter, the peter-men are better trained, the sneaks are cuter, an' the whole gang is better educated. I know it 'cause I have to keep track of 'em."

"How do you account for it?"

"It's easy enough. The guns come from the people, don't they? Well, the whole country is wiser to-day than it was twenty-five years ago, ain't it? Well, the guns have simply kept pace with the country. That's the whole story. If I'd start out now I'd have to begin at the beginnin' an' learn the whole business over again."

He paused again, and seemed to lose himself in his reminiscences. In a moment he looked up and smiled.

"They say 't a man can't begin anything fresh, an' make a success of it after he's reached sixty," he continued, "an' I guess I won't try. I'm satisfied; I've had my fling, an' it's over. I'd like to be back there with you in York this summer an' show you some o' the old dumps where I use to hang out, but I guess I can't make it. If you ever see anything that puzzles you, go to _____ , an' tell 'im you're a friend o' mine, an he'll explain the thing 'f he can. He knows as much about corruption as I do. Wherever you are, remember that if there's guns, cribs, an' Tenderloin in a town, there's crooked work goin' on. After you've located the guns an' the cribs, just dig down as deep as you can go, an' you'll get wise. That's an old gun's advice, an' the youngsters to-day can't give you any better."

I left him standing in the darkness on a railroad track. As my train pulled out, he shouted after me: "Don't forget what I said about Dr. Parkhurst," and then the train entered a tunnel, and he was lost to view.

Footnotes

1. Mother Mandelbaum was the most notorious "fencer" New York has ever had. She not only used the police in connection with her business, but was said to run the District Attorney's office as well. She made and lost hundreds of thousands of dollars.

2. Green-goods.

3. Penitentiary.

4. Safe.

5. A prisoner is put in the sweat-box when he is browbeaten by the police in order to make him divulge secrets in his possession.

What Comes of a Bad Name?

BY STEPHEN BURROUGHS

From *Memoirs of Stephen Burroughs* by Stephen Burroughs
(Hanover, New Hampshire: Benjamin True, 1798).

We have undoubtedly many inducements to regular, honest
and moral habits. I believe our liability to suspicion, when
outrages against morality occur, or the deeds of darkness are
developed without their author, and to the imputation of a
thousand irregularities and vices of which we are entirely innocent, is not the smallest. The world, in general, for the same
reason it calculates that the sun will rise tomorrow, because it
rose to-day, imputes to him, who has been once in a fault, the
commission of a hundred others.

This truth was very strongly proved to me, a few weeks ago,
in the trial of S.B. at the supreme court, at Worcester. Three
bills of indictment were presented against him for three as-
saults, upon three young women, with a felonious, though baf-
fled intent, each time to commit a rape. The charges were
solemn. A cloud of witnesses was gathered round him, to bear
testimony to the facts. The intended victims to his violence
were there also. The prisoner, on arraignment at the bar, plead
not guilty to the several indictments; and put himself on the
country for trial. S. the attorney-general managed the prosecution on the part of the commonwealth; and S. S. and L. were
advocates for the prisoner.

It was not to be wondered at, if the trial of the man, who
preached the sermon on the haymow to the Pelhamites, of
whom, while a prisoner on the Castle, many curious and di-
verting anecdotes had been told, and were still freshly remembered, had collected an uncommon assemblage of both sexes,
of women especially; when we add the nature of the offence to
the consideration.

The witnesses for the commonwealth were first examined.
The three girls who had suffered the injury for which the prisoner was arraigned were the most material. They told their sto-

ries so pertly that their declarations seemed to be rather mem-oieter than impromptu. I do not recollect all the particulars of their testimony, but could not help reckoning up the strong in-ducements the poor girls had to patch up as good a story as they could, to vindicate their own characters; enough of the circumstances of the transactions, through accident, or their own carelessness, had already leaked out, to render their virtue questionable; the world would make its own comments. The prisoner had been with them in private, and used them indeli-cately. If they had fallen unwilling victims to his lust, it was not their fault. But then, though their virtue remained as spotless as before, that indescribable something, that creature of our whims, that power to charm the men of this world, was weak-ened; and though they might still make as good members of the church, they would not prove such luscious brides.

One of the girls testified that the prisoner (one evening, af-ter he had dismissed his school, and after the other scholars were gone, she being left alone with him in the schoolhouse) attempted to persuade her to indelicate indulgences; took hold of her; behaved quite unseemly; and made some exertions to induce her to comply; not however, sufficient to require very strong efforts to prevent him, or cries to raise help, necessary; that at another time, afterwards, as she was returning home from school in the evening, in company with others, the pris-oner overtook them, was riding, and, as she had some length of way to walk, persuaded her to get up behind him, offering to carry her home; that having rode some distance with her, he stopped his horse, and took her from behind, and placed her before him; and behaved quite indecently; but that upon her resisting he desisted.

Another of the girls said the prisoner one day finding her in the barn, had attempted the same thing much in the same manner.

The third said he had enticed her one evening a few rods from the house, and they coming to a fence in their walk to-gether, he took her up in his arms and lifted her over, and pulled her down upon the ground, and attempted familiarities similar to the others; that on her making resistance, he desisted. She did not cry out; and I have forgot whether she, or any of the others, gave any reason why they did not.

This is quite an abridgment of the testimony; but I believe it contains all the material facts and circumstances, and is accurate and particular enough to furnish data for an opinion upon the nature of the offences.

The jury who tried the prisoner on the first indictment gave their verdict, *guilty.* The verdict of the second jury was *not guilty.* The attorney-general then entered a *nole prosequi* to the third indictment; and the prisoner was immediately arraigned to answer to two new bills, charging him with open and gross lewdness and lasciviousness. To them he plead guilty. And it appeared to me, his conduct amounted to no more in either of the cases; though the court, in stating the evidence, and giving their opinion to the jury on the two trials, were strongly set against the prisoner. It will at any rate, I believe, be allowed that if the prisoner merited the charge, he was, in one instance, quite original in the manner of the offence. Who but he would ever have thought of attempting to commit a rape on horseback? Surely, if he had succeeded, the world might well say he had fairly outquixoted Don Quixote himself. And if B. had really attempted what the girl said he did, a few evenings before, in the schoolhouse, her consenting to put herself, a second time, in his power, was no very strong proof of her discretion. At least, we must suppose, her jealousy at the schoolhouse had not occasioned her very serious alarms.

The affair at the barn, and that also at the fence, were transacted so in the very neighborhood of help, if it had been wanted, as to render the charge of his having attempted to commit a rape, in either of those cases, incredible. We cannot imagine any rational being would attempt to commit such an offence in a place where, if proper resistance was made and efforts used, he must certainly be discovered and prevented. And if such resistance was not made, he could not be concluded guilty of the crimes charged against him. I believe the conduct of the prisoner, in these instances, if impartially scanned (allowing that the girls told the truth) would be judged nothing more than so many resolute, earnest and persevering attempts to seduce them. With the generality of those who have heard of the conviction, it is possibly a matter of indifference, whether he was really guilty as charged or not. To them, the remembrance of many hard things the report has said of him, that he has been a prisoner on the Castle, would suggest the probability that he had been highly culpable in this instance, and produce their approbation of the verdict against him; especially if to these were added the consideration that the offence was at the lowest estimation of it, a gross indelicacy, a high outrage upon all the rules and principles of decorum and propriety.

It is difficult, in such a case as this, to extend to a prisoner at the bar, circumstanced as B. was, all the liberality of that excellent maxim which instructs us to presume the respondent innocent. Yet we are all equally entitled to justice; though undoubtedly our courts are more liable to do injustice to such a character as B. than to one that has fewer blemishes.

Is there no material difference between the crime of seduction and that of committing a rape? Neither of them are very praiseworthy, be sure; and each may be much aggravated by particular circumstances. But our legislators make a wide distinction; and the difference is very obvious to common sense. Is it material or not that we observe a distinction? I imagine the poor culprit, who is appointed to receive chastisement for his crime, would not feel indifferent whether he should be whipped or hanged for stealing.

Thus you see, sir, facts upon which you have to form an opinion relating to this very surprising trial. I have endeavored, so far as my Judgment would serve, to treat the characters concerned in this business with as much tenderness as the nature of a faithful narrative will admit. Wantonly to traduce a character is a species of conduct I wish by all means carefully to avoid; and where it has not been necessary, in order to give a true narrative of the facts which I promised, I have studiously suppressed any such emotion.

Possibly these matters may not appear to you as they have

done, and still do, to me. I know they cannot strike the mind of any in that feeling manner. I have made but a faint representation of them. I cannot communicate those ideas and sentiments, by writing, so fully as what they appear to my view by contemplation. However, we are apt to estimate the feelings of others by our own, and judge that they will view matters in the same manner as we do ourselves. In this estimation we often find ourselves mistaken. Hence, it is thought by many, that that person who feels most indifferent towards an object is in the best situation to form a true estimate, relating to that object.

I differ in sentiment with those who hold this doctrine. I know we are often hurried into error by the operation of our attachment to certain objects. Our passions, our appetites, and our zeal combine to produce this effect; hence, many conclude that it is necessary to feel perfectly indifferent towards an object in order to form a true estimation of its quality. We must feel interested in an object, either directly or indirectly, in order to call forth our attention towards it, sufficiently to examine its merits. When we feel indifferent towards an object, we pay no attention to it, and of course remain ignorant respecting it; therefore, are incapable of forming a just estimate concerning it.

A person who has no principle of humanity or compassion may hear of the exercise of cruelty. It is a report which finds no place in his feelings; he is indifferent as to its existence; therefore, we readily see that he would be an unequal judge as to the merits of the report.

Having a mind of sensibility, I know these matters will have their due operation on your feelings, and under this consideration I shall ever receive your observations with attention, and pay due regard to your ideas, upon any matter wherein you may think different from me.

That there is such a thing as right and wrong I believe is not called in question by any; and that we are all, in some measure, capable of judging with propriety upon this subject, is equally allowed. That we may, and are led astray many times, in forming an estimate of the principles of distributing justice, is a truth I shall by no means deny; but then we have all, I believe, a sufficient knowledge to distinguish upon the general principles of justice, at least, where we allow the operation of reason, without the embarrassments of prejudice.

When we find a private person injured by a public body, many circumstances are combined to lead the candid mind astray in the investigation of such a subject. Here error is most likely to take place. Popular clamor will be raised against the injured person; this is like the noise of the waters of Niagara; this swallows up the small voice of the individual.

We find the great Alexander, when the leading man of the world, committing acts of cruelty, injustice and oppression; a prospect of which, at this day, makes the blood curdle with horror; yet, those very actions were extolled in the most extravagant manner by his contemporary sycophants; and mankind gave him the most flattering encomiums, where they ought, upon the simple principles of right, to have execrated his conduct. This is a specimen of public opposition to private individuals, and the effects that follow, which I believe will hold good pretty generally, even in our days. Public characters are as liable to the malignant passions as other men; they are as prone, likewise, to be led astray, by the various causes that serve to lead mankind astray, as others; but when they find themselves in an error, they falsely suppose that it derogates from their dignity to acknowledge their error, and repair the injury which they have perpetrated, or even to have it suspected that they have been in an error. How false this system to the dictates of reason; how can the human character appear in a more exalted point of view than by showing a readiness to acknowledge and repair the injuries which our own misconduct has occasioned?

Tramps and Escapes

By Simeon Coy

From *The Great Conspiracy: A Complete History of the Famous Tally-Sheet Cases* by Simeon Coy (Indianapolis, 1889).

There are a goodly number of the human species termed "tramps," "bums," or "hobos," within the walls of the Northern Prison, and while they are the only class, perhaps, that there is no hope of reforming and therefore hardly worthy attention, I shall give a page or two pertaining to the illusions some people hold in regard to them.

In country towns they are considered authors of every crime, from robbing a hen-house to burglarizing a bank, and the word "tramp" in the bucolic mind is a synonym for all that is desperate, all that is wicked and all that is ingenious in crime. No greater fallacy prevails than the one that presumes these fellows capable of a great crime. It may be they are depraved enough, but the mere willingness on an individual's part to commit a crime is usually a long distance from its consummation. They are a worthless lot, as a general thing, ignorant, brutal and depraved, and any hope of reforming them is small.

A man with whom I conversed one day upon prisons and prisoners made the following remarks to me:

"Prisons! The best of them are no play-houses, but my experience has shown me that they would be less hard were it not for the tramps and plough-boys who come to them.

"These 'ducks,'" he went on, sarcastically, "have no heart for any dangerous violation of the prison discipline, such as escaping, but they are continually engaged in some senseless, petty, aggravating infraction of the rules, and the officers, without considering that these fellows are all of the same kidney, get sore on all convicts and treat all as a body as bad as these 'bums' are treated."

My inquiries regarding the class of men who are punished most frequently have corroborated the above remarks made by the man I have quoted, and who, by the way, is possessed of keen powers of observation.

Another impression anent the "hobos" is that they have a code of signals by means of which they can communicate with each other at a distance. This is also a fallacy. There is no tie that binds them together as a body, no understanding existing between them as a class. There is a peculiar jargon spoken by them that belongs to them alone. It consists in sounding the letters a, y, on the end of each word, and is not by any means hard to understand.

There is very little friendship or regard existing among them, though two or three, attracted to each other by some trait, may walk through an entire State, and when they part heartily despise each other. The following dialogue between two of them will illustrate how sympathetically they view a companion's misfortune:

Two of them meet, say in Toledo: "Hello, Shorty!" "Hello, Maggots!" "Where ye bin?" "West, on de U.P." "See Pig Iron any place?" "Yaas, him an' Yorkey is sloughed in de Hoosier State." "De h—l dey is, wot fur?" "Sluggin' a bloke wid a couplin' pin." "Dey git much stuff?" "Naw; seven cases." "How long is dey in fur?" "Five stretch apiece." "Five stretch fur seven cases! De bloody chumps." And this is the only sympathy expressed for the lamented disaster to "Pig Iron" and "Yorkey."

Taken as a whole, they are a bad lot, but there are not many of them who could justly be called dangerous, and if, among my readers there be any who imagine that a bevy of tramps on the outskirts of town means burglary and arson, rapine and murder during the night, they can rest assured no such deeds will come from Ishmael's favorite sons, the wandering "Hobo."

Before dismissing the subject of tramps and their doings I will relate an incident told me by a gentleman confined for a season in the northern retreat. This man is a typical bum, and is known from the rock-bound coast of Maine to the verdure-clad slopes of California as "Mulligan's Pug." Mulligan is by no means a bad-featured young man, and perhaps, trained in a different school from the one in which his boyhood was spent, he might have filled some post of usefulness in the world, though the wandering spirit was inborn in him, but, even so, he could have indulged it as a sailor, and I suggested as much to him one day.

"Nixey, boss. I made one vi'ge to Liverpool on a cow carrier from Quebec an' yer kin bet yer life I makes no more. De peck is starvation 'long side o' wot Murdock gives an' it was work, work, all de time," and a string of oaths emphasized his opinion of work of any kind, at any time or place.

But to the story Pug told me. His story, which I will try to give in his own aesthetic dialect:

"'Twas 'long in seventy-nine, me an' Squash Burke was a-movin' troo Ohio; de wedder was fine an' we was trampin' de country roads fur a change. One day we kim' to Bucyrus, Ohio, an' hevin' a few bones got full as geese an' spent 'em. We waked up in de mornin' feelin' purty tuff; bin layin' in de rain wot commenced to fall arter we was dead drunk, an' Squash, he say to me, 'Pug, go an' beg a few dimes an' some chuck.' I sez, 'You come wid me,' an' we started. It was a bad mornin' and de people fired us out as fast as dey kim to de door. It wus gettin' clust on ter noon 'fore we found a Samaritan. She was a nice-lookin' ol' party, an' all 'lone in de house. We axed her fur a meal an' she sez, 'Come right along in, boys, an' I'll git yer somethin'.' We went in; nice little house, everything neat an' clean, an' wile de ol' lady was a-cookin' de chuck, Squash he kep' a-makin' remarks like dis, 'Say, Pug, d'ye know dat ol' lady makes me think of my ol' maw; de same kind face, de same blue eyes, de same white hair,' an' knowin' de ol' soul was a-watchin' him he pumped up a few tears.

"'Pore feller,' says she, 'don't feel bad; better times 'll come p'raps, an' yer kin go back to your poor mudder.' It most made me laff, cos ye see I knows Squash's mudder; she's an' old lush.

"Wen de meal was near ready, Squash, who likes eggs, saw dere was none a cookin', an' de old bum say to de woman, nice an' purty: 'I begs yer pardin, mum; but I don't see no eggs on de table.' She looks up at dis statue o' gall, an' I think got skeered a little, fer ye know Squash is de ugliest lookin' tramp in de

States. 'I haven't an egg in de house,' she said at last. 'Too bad; I can't make a meal widout eggs,' sez Squash, and den he seemed to think a little an' sez: 'De rain has stopped, mum; so just give me some change an' de basket an' I'll run down to de store an' get some.' De old lady was par'lyzed, I reckin, for she never sed a word, but giv' de bum four bits an' a basket, an' off he went. I know'd he'd never come back no more, so I eat my chuck an' den moseyed off after Squash, an' found him in a boozin' ken drinkin' a geyser an' eatin' free lunch," and here Pug laughed as if it were a good joke to abuse the kindness of the old soul who had been good to them.

As a specimen of the cheek these loafers will display, the above anecdote is a fair sample, and it also displays the trait predominant in them, viz: if you treat them kindly they will think you a fool; treat them harshly, they will respect you. Such is my opinion from what I have seen of them in Michigan City.

Now, having disposed of the "lifers," the "accidentals" and the "hobos," I come to a class more interesting in every way, if more dangerous than the others—the professional crook. Within the grim walls of the Northern Prison has been the abiding place of many of the most noted and dangerous men this country has produced, men whose names are known and exploits mentioned wherever criminal life is discussed. At present there are not over fifty or so of noted professionals there, though in past years there have been many.

Frank Rande was at one time an inmate, a man whose desperate deeds rendered him a terror to a portion of Illinois, and who was captured in St. Louis only after he had slain two of the policemen making the arrest. This crime was ignored, however, as the State of Illinois had a prior claim on the distinguished murderer. He was taken to Illinois, tried for murder and sentenced to Joliet for life. A doubt as to his sanity existing in the minds of the jury was the only thing that saved him from the gallows. He died in Joliet after a murderous assault upon one of the prison officers, after being himself badly hurt. Suicide was what was claimed as the direct cause of his death, but "hung by the keepers" is the verdict of those familiar with the desperado's disposition. While in Michigan City his violent temper was manifested many times, but no serious results followed.

Among others who have a national reputation as dangerous crooks may be mentioned Mart Davis, who was associated with Paddy Guerin, Billy Burke and the redoubtable "Mollie" Matches in the Galesburg bank robbery. Jimmy Carroll, it is said, tarried there for a short season some years ago. Harry Floyd, Mike Wall and Billy Fairburn also "done a bit" for the daring robbery of an Indianapolis bank in 1878. This was one of the heaviest robberies ever committed in the State. During business hours, when the clerks of the bank were busy attending to their duties, the gang of crooks entered and placed themselves in the most suitable positions for screening the "sneak," or performing pal, from observation. The latter, when he entered, carried in his hand an ordinary looking sample case, and after a quick glance about the bank and getting signals from his confederates, placed his case on the floor near the teller's window, and reaching over grabbed packages of currency amounting to nearly $25,000. The excitement and furore the crime created is still remembered by many of the citizens of the city. But there are very few, if any, who know that the man who actually stole the money was concealed for five days in the house of a policeman attached to the city force. That this is true I know, from information given me by a crook who was serving a short sentence during my sojourn in the Northern Prison, and among other things he told me of the robbery. I have no doubt he was closely associated with the thieves at the time it was committed. The oddest fact in connection with the matter is that the actual thief was never arrested for the affair, but the others, or a portion of them, Floyd *alias* Southgate, Fairburn and Wall, served their time for the crime.

Many others of equal note might be named, but they are gone, and their subsequent lives are no doubt written in the annals of crime.

In more recent years there have been but few, comparatively speaking, of such crooks in the Prison North. Bill Hoolihan and his partner, Gib Yost, were sent there in 1884 for a jewelry robbery of some magnitude. Hoolihan received a sentence of two years and Yost fourteen. The former served his time. Yost died in prison some two years ago. Thus ended the career of a great criminal.

"Red" Hyler, the "prince of hotel thieves," completed a five years term before I left, and he expressed his determination to lead an honest life in future. May he do so, for convict and criminal though he be, few men possess more manliness or a better heart than quiet "Red."

Among the most noted who still abide within the walls of the Prison North, is Harry Underwood, whose exploits as lieutenant to the daring road agent, Jane Bass, are well known to the police east and west. A better natured, truer-hearted man with his friends can not be found; with his enemies he is not quite so genial and generous, it is said.

Next to Underwood comes "Walk" Hammond, who for eighteen long months has fought a hard, grim fight with death, and kept him at bay by the sheer force of his iron will and courage. That his days are numbered, there can be no doubt, for consumption holds him in its relentless grip, and his life, and the death of poor Walk, when it comes, will point a moral to all young men inclined to go wrong, a lesson never to be forgotten. In the long months of my own incarceration, I was daily brought in contact with this man, whose life has held so much that is thrilling and romantic, desperate and deadly, too, perhaps, that I can hardly believe it, and I have often wondered if society, against which such men have declared war, does not often manufacture its own pariahs. Hammond's youth gave no indication of the spirit, that in later years, moved him to do deeds that placed him under the ban of society. In his boyhood, almost, he entered the army, and served faithfully through the war, and bore his full share of wounds and hardships. When peace came, he went back to his home on a farm, a little wild and reckless, perhaps—for the years of camp and battle made many such—and went to work. For years after he was an engineer on the JM & I.R.R. His first appearance as a criminal was as a partner of the Reno boys, whose bold robberies startled the country at the time, and who were hunted down by that king of detectives Allan Pinkerton. Just what Hammond's degree of guilt or innocence in the robberies perpetrated by the Reno gang was, I do not know. He was convicted and sent to the Southern Prison, and no doubt that ruined him for any future usefulness. Since then he has figured as one of the greatest criminals in the land. He has been a confederate of such men as Bill Boyd, Old Man Mills, Peter McCartney, and other dangerous makers of spurious money, and yet his present conviction is for a crime of which I verily believe him innocent, and which pointedly illustrates the truth of the saying, "give a dog a bad name," etc. As I write, this man lies at the point of death. Only a short time can elapse ere he goes to the judgment of a higher court than those which have made his life a desert on earth. I can remember a thousand conversations I have had with him, remembering how patient under great trials and suffering he has been, how true and steadfast to his friends; thinking also of his iron will and hardy courage, his strong intellect and wide knowledge of men and the world—I ask myself if the law does not deal harshly many times with those who go astray. What do any of us know of the temptations that must beset such a man, and how can any of us gauge or understand the influences that drive him into the tribe of Ishmael? Is there, after all, a Fate, that marks out the path each human soul must travel and out of which no human power or mortal will can turn him?

Following Underwood and Hammond, the names of Henry Tettman and Reddy Jackson, the Attica postoffice robbers, may be mentioned as among the clever professionals in the Prison North. Also Bob Henry and his partner Fox, both famous bunko men. The same may be said in regard to Charlie Ellison, Red Gordon and Tad Newman, and no doubt there are fifty others whose names I can not recall.

These men, as a rule, give but little trouble to the officers, though the greatest vigilance is always exercised in watching them. These are the men from whom the authorities expect attempts to escape, but the system of surveillance is such it is very seldom even an attempt is made, and rarely, indeed, is one successful. In fact there has been no escape for years that could be classed as such. There have been runaways, it is true, but only in the cases where the fugitives were "trusties" and worked outside of the walls.

The most extensive break ever planned under Warden Murdock's administration was the one led by John Kennedy. The plan was to capture the night guard in the cell house, and keys having been fitted and made that would open the door leading into the guard room, where the other guards were, capture all hands and let all who cared to go have their freedom. Kennedy performed his part, but there was lack of courage on the part of his confederates, and the guard was able to give an alarm and arouse the prison force ere he was captured by the desperate gang, and the break was quelled by the wounding of Kennedy.

The man who needed the most vigilant watching of any convict within the walls was Pete McCartney, the great counterfeiter, and though he was kept under close surveillance he came very near making his escape on two occasions. In the first years of Pete's incarceration there was a man who was allowed to keep a lot of rabbits and chickens in one corner of the yard. This man was old Pete's route home, and with the adroitness and cunning he possessed above all men, the old coney man succeeded in coming to an understanding with he of the rabbits, and it was to the effect that the latter was to tunnel from beneath his rabbit hutch under the prison wall, which he could very easily do, as he was not looked upon with suspicion by the officers, and his movements would always be screened from the sight of the wall guard, beneath whose very feet the work went on.

After a long interval of cunning labor the work was completed, and nothing prevented the exit of the two worthies; nothing, at least, but the failure of Pete to produce the sum of money which he had promised the rabbit man. "When we get out and away all right, you shall have it," said the wily Pete to his tool. But this was not satisfactory to the gentleman, so he put Pete off for the time, promising to accompany him the next afternoon; then, wishing no doubt to test the utility of his labor, he made use of the tunnel and escaped alone, leaving Pete to curse and fume at the trick his tool had played him. Poor tool! He was but a dull instrument after all, as his recapture followed closely upon his escape, and his after life in the prison was not a bed of roses. But Pete, in no manner discouraged at the failure of the scheme that was foiled by his own distrust of his tool, or his own cupidity, set about the execution of another plan to escape.

The cell-house entrance at that time was through a single massive door, hard to break or batter, but simple enough to pick, or, still better, make a key to fit. At 9 o'clock, each night the guard (there was but one in each cell-house then) made his round of the ranges to see that all lights were extinguished and the convicts in bed. This and other details Pete, of course, was acquainted with. Having succeeded in making a key to fit the outer door of the cell-house, and in the meantime having sawed through the bars of his cell, he only waited a favorable night to make the attempt. He had also managed, in some way, to secure an impression of a tower key and had supplied himself with a key to open the same, and would surely have succeeded in escaping had it not been for an accident. The night he wished came at last, dark, windy and rainy, and when the guard ascended the ranges at the 9 o'clock bell Pete slipped from his cell to the entrance door, turned the bolt, and was within a yard of freedom when a gust of wind caught the half-opened door and closed it with a bang. That caused the guard to pause on his round and he saw Pete and commanded him to surrender, which he did, and was returned to his cell again.

It was on the following morning, while he was in the office to answer for his attempt to escape, that Warden Murdock took a fancy to see the inside of the truss which he wore, and Mr. Murdock's curiosity or shrewdness was rewarded by finding a large amount of money, snugly packed away in the old man's supporter. This was Pete's last attempt to escape, or at least the last of which the officers had knowledge, but it's doubtful if there passed a single day of his sentence in which he did not plan and scheme to get away.

Only a few months after his release from the Northern Prison he was arrested in New Orleans for passing counterfeit money, and is now in Columbus prison serving another long sentence, and where he will, no doubt, end his life; a life that has been remarkable for the immense sums of money he has had through the means of counterfeiting, and also for the many escapes he has made at various times, but he is getting old now and his days are about over.

Speaking of escapes recalls the daring effort made by Frank Whiting and John Havens, the two Indianapolis desperadoes, to avoid the penalty of their crimes. They made three attempts at divers times, the first two being foiled before anything like success was promised; the third and last was the boldest and nearest to success, and happened in this way:

Every morning a switch engine enters the yard to pull out freight cars, loaded or unloaded the day previous, by the various contractors. When the engine is ready to leave the yard, a signal is given and the big gate swings open. Directly over the gate stand two guards, heavily armed, and to pass them unhurt would be a miracle. There is, perhaps, one chance in a thousand, and this one chance Whiting and Havens took. Accordingly, one morning in September, 1887, they rushed from the shoe-shop in which they worked, brushing aside everyone who attempted to stop them, and sprung upon the engine when it was within twenty yards of the open gate. With loud cries and threats they drove the engineer and firemen from the cab. Whiting grasped lever and throttle, threw one ahead and pulled the other wide open, and—overdid it—the engine giving one great bound and stopping. By the time they had sprung upon the engine, old Charlie Young, a phlegmatic German, who guarded the wall, had taken aim at the two desperadoes and fired a load of buckshot; a moment later and the contents of the second barrel of his gun went crashing through the roof of the cab, and one bullet found lodgment in the breast of young Whiting, an inch above his heart, and he fell dead, still grasping throttle and lever. Havens sprang from the engine and started for the woods, but was speedily re-captured. He had sprained his ankle, and had also been grazed on the head by a bullet.

This ended an attempt that for desperate hardihood and reckless courage stands unsurpassed in the annals of prison escapes.

Self-Preservation

By John Wesley Hardin

From *The Life of John Wesley Hardin As Written By Himself* (Seguin, Texas: Smith & Moore, 1896).

The State tried to prove a conspiracy, but utterly failed in this, hence the prosecution ought to have fallen through. The State proved themselves that Charley Webb had fired at me twice before I drew my pistol, or that I drew and fired as he was shooting his second shot.

The simple fact is that Charles Webb had really come over from his own county that day to kill me, thinking I was drinking and at a disadvantage. He wanted to kill me to keep his name, and he made his break on me like an assassin would. He fired his first shot at my vitals when I was unprepared, and who blames a man for shooting under such conditions? I was at a terrible disadvantage in my trial. I went before the court on a charge of murder without a witness. The cowardly mob had either killed them or run them out of the county. I went to trial in a town in which three years before my own brother and cousins had met an awful death at the hands of a mob. Who of my readers would like to be tried under these circumstances? On that jury that tried me sat six men whom I knew to be directly implicated in my brother's death. No, my readers, I have served twenty-five years for the killing of Webb, but know ye that there is a God in high heaven who knows that I did not shoot Charles Webb through malice, nor through anger, nor for money, but to save my own life.

True, it is almost as bad to kill as to be killed. It drove my father to an early grave; it almost distracted my mother; it killed my brother Joe and my cousins Tom and William; it left my brother's widow with two helpless babes; Mrs. Anderson lost her son Ham, and Mrs. Susan Barrickman lost her husband, to say nothing of the grief of countless others. I do say, however, that the man who does not exercise the first law of nature—

that of self preservation—is not worthy of living and breathing the breath of life.

The jury gave me twenty-five years in the penitentiary and found me guilty of murder in the second degree. I appealed the case. The Rangers took me back to Austin to await the result of my appeal. Judge White affirmed the decision of the lower court, and they took me back to Comanche in the latter part of September, 1878, where I received my sentence of twenty-five years with hard labor.

While I was in that Austin jail, I had done everything in my power to escape. The cells were made of good material and in fact the jail was a good one, with one set of cages on top of the others, separated by sheet iron. I soon got so I could make a key that would unlock my cell door and put me in the runaround. I made a key to unlock that, and now all I had to do was climb to the window and saw one of the bars. I could then easily escape. But some "trusties" found out the scheme and gave it away to the jailer, who placed a guard inside the jail day and night. Thus it became impossible for me to do the work in the window, though I had the key to the cell and the runaround.

There were from sixty to ninety prisoners in that jail all the time, and at least fifty of these stood ready to inform on me any time. There was the trouble about getting out.

In that jail I met some noted men. Bill Taylor, George Gladden, John Ringo, Manning Clements, Pipes and Herndon of the Bass gang, John Collins, Jeff Ake, and Brown Bowen.

After receiving my sentence at Comanche, they started with me to Huntsville, shackled to John Maston, a blacksmith of Comanche convicted of attempting to murder and under two years' sentence. This man afterwards committed suicide by jumping from the upper story in the building to a rock floor, where he was dashed to pieces. Nat Mackey, who was sentenced for seventeen years for killing a man with a rock, was chained to Davenport, who had a sentence of five years for horse stealing. Thus there were four prisoners chained by two's in a wagon and guarded by a sheriff and company of Rangers.

Of course, great crowds would flock from everywhere to see the notorious John Wesley Hardin, from the hoary-headed farmer to the little maid hardly in her teens.

On one occasion a young lady told me she had come over to where we were passing the day before and would not have missed seeing me for $100. I asked her if she was satisfied now. She said, "Oh, yes; I can tell everybody I have seen the notorious John Wesley Hardin, and he is so handsome!"

What the Burglar Faces

By Light-Fingered Jim

From *The Autobiography of a Thief,* Recorded by Hutchins Hapgood
(New York: Fox, Duffield & Co., 1903).

For a long time I took Sheenie Annie's advice and did not do
any night work. It is too dangerous, the come-back is too sure,
you have to depend too much on the nerve of your pals, the
"bits" are too long; and it is very difficult to square it. But as
time went on I grew bolder. I wanted to do something new, and
get more dough. My new departure was not, however, entirely
due to ambition and the boldness acquired by habitual success.
After a gun has grafted for a long time his nervous system becomes affected, for it is certainly an exciting life. He is then
very apt to need a stimulant. He is usually addicted to either
opium or chloral, morphine or whiskey. Even at this early period
I began to take a little opium, which afterwards was one of the
main causes of my constant residence in stir, and was really the
wreck of my life, for when a grafter is doped he is inclined to
be very reckless. Perhaps if I had never hit the hop I would not
have engaged in the dangerous occupation of a burglar.

I will say one thing for opium, however. That drug never
makes a man careless of his personal appearance. He will go to
prison frequently, but he will always have a good front, and will
remain a self-respecting thief. The whiskey dip, on the other
hand, is apt to dress carelessly, lose his ambition and eventually
to go down and out as a common "bum."

I began night work when I was about twenty years old, and
at first I did not go in for it very heavily. Big Jack, Jerry, Ed and I
made several good touches in Mt. Vernon and in hotels at summer resorts and got sums ranging from two hundred to twenty-
seven hundred dollars. We worked together for nearly a year
with much success and only an occasional fall, and these we succeeded in squaring. Once we had a shooting-match which made
me a little leary. I was getting out the window with my swag,
when a shot just grazed my eye. I nearly decided to quit then,

but, I suppose because it was about that time I was beginning to take opium, I continued with more boldness than ever.

One night Ed, a close pal of mine, was operating with me out in Jersey. We were working in the rear of a house and Ed was just shinning up the back porch to climb in the second story window, when a shutter above was thrown open and, without warning, a pistol shot rang out.

Down came Ed, falling like a log at my feet.

"Are you hurt?" said I.

"Done!" said he, and I saw it was so.

Now a man may be nervy enough, but self-preservation is the first rule of life. I turned and ran at the top of my speed across two back yards, then through a field, then over a fence into what seemed a ploughed field beyond. The ground was rough and covered with hummocks, and as I stumbled along I suddenly tripped and fell ten feet down into an open grave. The place was a cemetery, though I had not recognized it in the darkness. For hours I lay there trembling, but nobody came and I was safe. It was not long after that, however, that something did happen to shake my nerve, which was pretty good. It came about in the following way.

A jeweler, who was a well-known "fence," put us on to a place where we could get thousands. He was one of the most successful "feelers-out" in the business. The man who was my pal on this occasion, Dal, looked the place over with me and though we thought it a bit risky, the size of the graft attracted us. We had to climb up on the front porch, with an electric light streaming down on us.

I had reached the porch when I got the well-known signal of danger. I hurriedly descended and asked Dal what was the matter.

"Jim," he said, "there's somebody off there, a block away."

We investigated, and you can imagine how I felt when we found nothing but an old goat. It was a case of Dal's nerves, but the best of us got nervous at times.

I went to the porch again and opened the window with a putty knife (made of the rib of a woman's corset), when I got the "cluck" again and hastily descended, but again found it was Dal's imagination

Then I grew hot, and said "You have knocked all the nerve out of me, for sure."

"Jim," he replied, "I ain't feeling good."

Was it a premonition? He wanted to quit the job, but I wouldn't let him. I opened up on him. "What!" I said. "You are willing to steal one piece of jewelry and take your chance of going to stir, but when we get a good thing that would land us in Easy Street the rest of our lives, you weaken!"

Dal was quiet, and his face unusually pale. He was a good fellow, but his nerve was gone. I braced him up, however, and told him we'd get the "éclat" the third time, sure. Then climbing the porch the third time, I removed my shoes, raised the window again, and had just struck a light when a revolver was pressed on my head. I knocked the man's hand up, quick, and jumped. As I did so I heard a cry and then the beating of a policeman's stick on the sidewalk.

I ran, with two men after me, and came to the gateway of a yard, where I saw a big bloodhound chained to his kennel. He growled savagely, but it was neck or nothing, so I patted his head just as though I were not shaking with fear, slipped down on my hands and knees and crept into his dog-house. Why didn't he bite me? Was it sympathy? When my pursuers came up, the owner of the house, who had been aroused by the cries, said: "He is not here. This dog would eat him up." When the police saw the animal they were convinced of it too.

A little while later I left my friend's kennel. It was four o'-clock in the morning and I had no shoes on and only one dollar and sixty cents in my pocket. I sneaked through the back window of the first house I saw, stole a pair of shoes and eighty dollars from a room where a man and his wife were sleeping. Then I took a car. Knowing that I was still being looked for, I wanted to get rid of my hat, as a partial disguise. On the seat with me was a working man asleep. I took his old soft hat, leaving my new derby by his side, and also took his dinner pail. Then when I left the car I threw away my collar and necktie, and reached New York, disguised as a workingman. The next day the papers told how poor old Dal had been arrested. Everything that had happened for weeks was put on him.

A week later Dal was found dead in his cell, and I believe he did the Dutch act (suicide), for I remember one day, months before that fatal night, Dal and I were sitting in a politician's saloon, when he said to me:

"Jim, do you believe in heaven?"

"No," said I.

"Do you believe in hell?" he asked.

"No," said I.

"I've got a mind to find out," he said quickly, and pointed a big revolver at his teeth. One of the guns in the saloon said: "Let him try it," but I knocked the pistol away, for something in his manner made me think seriously he would shoot.

"You poor brute," I said to him. "I'll put your ashes in an urn some day and write 'Dear Old Saturday Night' for an epitaph for you; but it isn't time yet."

It did not take many experiences like the above to make me very leary of night work; and I went more slowly for some time. I continued to dip, however, more boldly than ever and to do a good deal of day work; in which comparatively humble graft the servant girls used to help us out considerably. This class of women never interested me as much as the sporting characters, but we used to make good use of them; and sometimes they amused us.

I remember an entertaining episode which took place while Harry, a pal of mine at the time, and I, were going with a couple of these hardworking Molls. Harry was rather inclined to be a sure-thing grafter; and after my recent dangerous adventures I tolerated that class more than was customary with me. Indeed, if Harry had been the real thing I would have cut him dead; as it was he came near enough to the genuine article to make me despise him in my ordinary mood. But, as I say, I was uncommonly leary just at that time.

He and I were walking in Stuyvesant Square when we met a couple of these domestic slaves. With a "hello," we rang in on them, walked them down Second Avenue and had a few drinks all around. My girl told me whom she was working with. Thinking there might be something doing I felt her out further, with a view to finding where in the house the stuff lay. Knowing the Celtic character thoroughly, I easily got the desired information. We took the girls into Bonnell's Museum, at Eighth Street and Broadway, and saw a howling border melodrama, in which wild Indians were as thick as Mollbuzzers in 1884. Mary Anne, who was my girl, said she should tell her mistress about the beautiful play; and asked for a program. They were all out, and so I gave her an old one, of another play, which I had in my pocket. We had a good time and made a date with them for another meeting in two weeks from that night; but before the appointed hour we had beat Mary Anne's mistress out of two hundred dollars worth of silverware, easily obtained, thanks to the information I had received from Anne. When we met the girls again, I found Mary Anne in a great state of indignation; I was afraid she was "next" to our being the burglars, and came near falling through the floor. But her rage, it seemed, was about the play. She had told her mistress about the wild Indian melodrama she had seen and then had shown her the program of *The Banker's Daughter.*

"But there is no such thing as an Indian in *The Banker's Daughter,*" her mistress had said. "I fear you are deceiving me, Mary Anne, and that you have been to some low place on the Bowery."

The other servants in the house got next and kidded Mary Anne almost to death about Indians and *The Banker's Daughter.* After I had quieted her somewhat she told me about the burglary that had taken place at her house, and Harry and I were much interested. She was sure the touch had been made by two "naygers" who lived in the vicinity.

It was shortly after this incident that I beat Blackwell's Island out of three months. A certain "heeler" put me on to a disorderly house where we could get some stones. I had everything "fixed." The "heeler" had arranged it with the copper on the beat, and it seemed like a sure thing; although the Madam, I understood, was a good shot and had plenty of nerve. My accomplice, the heeler, was a sure thing grafter, who had selected me because I had the requisite nerve and was no squealer. At two o'clock in the morning a trusted pal and I ascended from the back porch to the Madam's bedroom. I had just struck a match, when I heard a female voice say, "What are you doing there?" and a bottle, fired at my head, banged up against the wall with a crash. I did not like to alarm women, and so I made my "gets" out the window, over the fence, and into another street, where I was picked up by a copper, on general principles.

The Madam told him that the thief was over six feet tall and had a fierce black mustache. As I am only five feet seven inches and was smoothly shaven, it did not seem like an identification; although when she saw me she changed her note, and swore I was the man. The copper, who knew I was a grafter, though he did not think I did that kind of work, nevertheless took me to the stationhouse, where I convinced two wardmen that I had been arrested unjustly. When I was led before the magistrate in the morning, the copper said the lady's description did not tally with the short, red-haired and freckled thief before his Honor. The policemen all agreed, however, that I was a notorious grafter, and the magistrate, who was not much of a lawyer, sent me to the Island for three months on general principles.

I was terribly sore, for I knew I had been illegally treated. I felt as much a martyr as if I had not been guilty in the least; and I determined to escape at all hazards; although my friends told me I would be released any day; for certainly the evidence against me had been insufficient.

After I had been on the Island ten days I went to a friend, who had been confined there several months, and said: "Eddy, I have been unjustly convicted for a crime I committed—such was my way of putting it—and I am determined to make my elegant (escape), come what will. Do you know the weak spots of this dump?"

He put me "next," and I saw there was a chance, a slim one, if a man could swim and didn't mind drowning. I found another pal, Jack Donovan, who, like me, could swim like a fish; he was desperate too, and willing to take any chance to see New York. Five or six of us slept together in one large cell, and on the night selected for our attempt, Jack and I slipped into a compartment where about twenty short term prisoners were kept. Our departure from the other cell, from which it was very difficult to escape after once being locked in for the night, was not noticed by the night guard and his trusty because our pals in the cell answered to our names when they were called. It was comparatively easy to escape from the large room where the short term men were confined. Into this room, too, Jack and I had taken tools from the quarry during the daytime.

It was twelve o'clock on a November night when we made our escape. We took ropes from the canvas cot, tied them together, and lowered ourselves to the ground on the outside, where we found bad weather, rain and hail. We were unable to obtain a boat, but secured a telegraph pole, rolled it into the water, and set off with it for New York. The terrific tide at Hellgate soon carried us well into the middle of Long Island Sound, and when we had been in the water half an hour, we were very cold and numb, and began to think that all was over. But neither of us feared death. All I wanted was to save enough money to be cremated; and I was confident my friends would see to that. I don't think fear of death is a common trait among grafters. Perhaps it is lack of imagination; more likely, however, it is because they think they won't be any the worse off after death.

Still, I was not sorry when a wrecking boat suddenly popped our way. The tug did not see us, and hit Jack's end of the pole a hard blow that must have shaken him off. I heard him holler "Save me," and I yelled too. I didn't think anything about capture just then. All my desire to live came back to me.

I was pulled into the boat. The captain was a good fellow. He was "next" and only smiled at my lies. What was more to the purpose he gave me some good whiskey, and set me ashore in Jersey City. Jack was drowned. All through life I have been used to losing a friend suddenly by the wayside; but I have always felt sad when it happened. And yet it would have been far better for me if I had been picked out for an early death. I guess poor Jack was lucky.

Certainly there are worse things than death. Through these three years of continual and for the most part successful graft, I had known a man named Henry Fry whose story is one of the saddest. If he had been called off suddenly as Jack was, he would certainly have been deemed lucky by those who knew; for he was married to a bad woman. He was one of the most successful box-men (safeblowers) in the city, and made thousands, but nothing was enough for his wife. She used to say, when he would put twelve hundred dollars in her lap, "This won't meet expenses. I need one thousand dollars more." She was unfaithful to him, too, and with his friends. When I go to a matinee and see a lot of sleek, fat, inane looking women, I wonder who the poor devils are who are having their life blood sucked out of them. Certainly it was so with Henry, or Henny, as we used to call him.

One day, I remember, we went down the Sound with a well-known politician's chowder party, and Henny was with us. Two weeks earlier New York had been startled by a daring burglary. A large silk-importer's place of business was entered and his safe, supposed to be burglar-proof, was opened. He was about to be married, and his valuable wedding presents, which were in the safe, and six thousand dollars worth of silk, were stolen. It was Henny and his pals who had made the touch, but on this beautiful night on the Sound, Henny was sad. We were sitting on deck, as it was a hot summer night, when Henny jumped off his camp-stool and asked me to sing a song. I sang a sentimental ditty, in my tenor voice, and then Henny took me to the side of the boat, away from the others.

"Kid," he said, "I feel trouble coming over me."

"Cheer up," I replied. "You're a little down-hearted, that's all."

"I wish to God," he said, "I was like you."

I pulled out a five dollar bill and a two dollar bill and remarked: "I've got just seven dollars to my name."

He turned to me and said:

"But you are happy. You don't let anything bother you."

Henny did not drink as a rule; that was one reason he was such a good box-man, but on this occasion we had a couple of drinks, and I sang "I love but one." Then Henny ordered champagne, grew confidential, and told me his troubles.

"Kid" he said, "I've got thirty five hundred dollars on me. I have been giving my wife a good deal of money, but don't know what she does with it. In sixty days I have given her three thousand dollars, and she complains about poverty all the time."

Henny had a nice flat of seven or eight rooms; he owed nothing and had no children. He said he was unable to find any bank books in his wife's trunk, and was confident she was not laying the money by. She did not give it to her people, but even borrowed money from her father, a well-to-do builder.

Two days after the night of the excursion, one of Henny's pals in the silk robbery went into a gin mill, treated everybody, and threw a one thousand dollar bill down on the bar.

Grafters, probably more than others, like this kind of display. It is the only way to rise in their society. A Central Office detective saw this little exhibition, got into the grafter's confidence and weeded him out a bit. A night or two afterwards Henny was in bed at home, when the servant girl, who was in love with Henny, and detested his wife because she treated her husband so badly (she used to say to me, "She ain't worthy to tie his shoe string") came to the door and told Henny and his wife that a couple of men and a policeman in uniform were inquiring for him. Henny replied sleepily that they were friends of his who had come to buy some stones; but the girl was alarmed. She knew that Henny was crooked and feared that those below meant him no good. She took the canvas turnabout containing burglar's tools which hung on the wall near the bed, and pinned it around her waist, under her skirt, and then admitted the three visitors.

The sergeant said to Henny, who had dressed himself, "You are under suspicion for the silk robbery." Yet there was, as is not uncommon, a "but," which is as a rule a monetary consideration. Henny knew that the crime was old, and, as he

thought his "fence" was safe, he did not see how there could
be a come-back. So he did not take the hint to shell out, and
worked the innocent con. But those whose business it is to
watch the world of prey put two and two together, and were
"next" that Henny and his mob had pulled off the trick. So
they searched the house, expecting to find, if not *éclat,* at least
burglar's tools; for they knew that Henny was at the top of the
ladder, and that he must have something to work with. While
the sergeant was going through Henny's trunk, one of the fly-
men fooled with the pretty servant girl. She jumped, and a pair
of turners fell on the floor. It did not take the flyman long to
find the whole kit of tools. Henny was arrested, convicted, and
sent to Sing Sing for five years. While in prison he became insane, his delusion being that he was a funny man on the Detroit Free Press, which he thought was owned by his wife.

I never discovered what Henny's wife did with the money
she had from him. When I last heard of her she was married to
another successful grafter, whom she was making unhappy
also. In a grafter's life a woman often takes the part of the
avenger of society. She turns against the grafters their own
weapons, and uses them with more skill, for no man can graft
like a woman.

Real Facts About the Northfield, Minnesota Bank Robbery

RELATED BY THOMAS COLEMAN "COLE" YOUNGER, from *Convict Life at the Minnesota State Prison* (St. Paul, Minnesota: W.C. Heilbron, 1909).

"In telling the story of the Northfield bank robbery and its frightful results I have only to say that there is no heroism in outlawry, and that the man who sows is sure to reap. After Lee surrendered I tried my best to live at peace with the world and earn a livelihood. I'd been made a guerrilla by a provocation that few men could have resisted. My father had been cruelly murdered, my mother had been hounded to death, my entire family had been tormented and all my relatives plundered and imprisoned.

"From the mass of rubbish that has been written about the guerrilla there is little surprise that the popular conception of him should be a fiendish, bloodthirsty wretch.

"Yet he was in many cases, if not in most, a man who had been born to better things and who was made what he was by such outrages as Osceola, Palmyra and by a hundred raids in less famous but not less infamous, that were made by Kansans into Missouri during the war.

"When the war ceased those of the guerrillas who were not hung or shot or pursued by posses till they found the hand of man turned against them at every step, settled down to become good citizens in the peaceful walks of life, and the survivors of Quantrell's band may be pardoned, in view of the black paint that has been devoted to them, in calling attention to the fact that of the members of Quantrell's band who have since been entrusted with public place, not one has everbetrayed his trust.

"As for myself and brothers I wish to emphasize that we made an honest attempt to return to normal life at the close of the war, and had we been permitted to do so the name of

Younger would never have been connected with the crimes that were committed in the period immediately following the war.

"That my life was good or clean I do not assert. But such as it was, it was forced upon me by conditions over which I had no control. Before final judgment is passed upon the men of my kind who were with me in those days I ask that the fact be considered that we were born in days when hatred was the rule and reared among scenes of violence.

"But I have been accused of many crimes of which I have not been guilty, and I am willing to take my oath that the crimes that were charged against me in Missouri were not mine. Never in all my life had I anything to do with any of the bank robberies in the state of Missouri which had been charged against myself and brothers.

"In the fall of 1868 my brothers, Jim and Bob, went with me to Texas. The next two or three years we spent in an honest life, my sister joining us and keeping house for us at Syene, Dallas County. In 1870 and 1871 Jim was deputy sheriff in Dallas County. He and Bob sang in the church choir. At that time Bob, who was only 17, fell in love with one of the young ladies in the village.

"I went down to Louisiana, and the story was told that I killed five men and shot five others because I had been robbed by a lot of crooked cattlemen. There is just this much truth about this incident: There was a crooked race, with me as the victim. After the race I fought a duel, but not over the race.

"The duel was forced upon me by a man named Captain James White. He circulated a scandalous tale about the young woman Bob was in love with. I sent word to him that he would have to apologize or fight. After the race I referred to White and I went to a neighboring plantation and fought it out. At the first shot his right arm was shattered at the shoulder. When he thought he was dying he apologized and admitted that he had circulated the story for the purpose of forcing a fight upon me.

"It was about this time that the Kansas City fair was robbed. This was charged against the Younger brothers, although not one of us had anything to do with it. Bob felt so keenly the notoriety that resulted from my duel and from the stories of the Kansas City robbery that he left Dallas, and later Jim and I followed him. About this time my brother John, who was only 14 years old when the war closed, was forced into a quarrel and murdered as wantonly as a man was ever murdered in the history of the west.

"When I was on the Pacific slope Missouri adopted the famous Drake constitution, which prohibited Confederate soldiers and sympathizers from practicing any profession, preaching the gospel or doing many other things under a penalty of a fine of not less than $500 or imprisonment for not less than six months. One section of this constitution gave amnesty to Union soldiers for all they had done after January 1, 1861, but held Confederates responsible for what they had done either as citizens or soldiers.

"The result of this was the persecution of all men who were not friendly with the carpet-bag administration following the war and there was no mercy shown to any of them. After a few days of seeing my friends and old comrades hounded and imprisoned I saw there was nothing left for me to do but gather together with those that were left and do the best we could.

"In passing swiftly over the scenes of violence in which we took part, I will take up the Northfield case by saying that we had decided to find a good bank, make a big haul, get away with the money, leave the country and start life anew in some foreign land.

"We were told that General Benjamin F. Butler had a big lot of money in the First National bank at Northfield, and that A.A. Ames, son-in-law of Butler, who had been a carpet-bag governor of Mississippi after the war, had a lot there also. We were not very friendly to Butler because of his treatment of Southerners during the war, and accordingly decided to make a raid on the Northfield bank.

"My brothers, Jim and Bob, Clell Miller, Bill Chadwell and three men named Pitts, Woods and Howard, were those who decided to take up the expedition. This was in the middle of August, and we spent a week in Minneapolis picking up what information we could about Northfield and the bank and playing poker. Then we passed another week in St. Paul, also looking for information as to the amount of money and the precautions taken in the bank to take care of it.

"Chadwell, Pitts, Bob and myself procured horses at St. Peter, where we stayed long enough to break them and to train them for the hard riding to which we knew they would be submitted later on. It was at St. Peter that I made the acquaintance of a little girl who afterwards was one of the most earnest workers for our parole.

"A little tot then, she said she could ride a horse, too, and reaching down, I lifted her up before me, and we rode up and down. I asked her her name and she said it was 'Horace Greeley Perry,' and I replied:

"'No wonder you're such a little tot with such a great name.'

"'I won't always be little,' she replied. 'I'm going to be a great big girl and be a newspaper man like papa.'

"'Will you still be my sweetheart then, and be my friend?' I asked her, and she declared she would, a promise I was to remind her of years later under circumstances of which I did not dream then.

"Many years afterward with a party of visitors to the prison came a girl, perhaps 16, who registered in full, 'Horace Greeley Perry.'

"I knew there could not be two women with such a name in the world. and I reminded her of her promise, a promise which she did not remember, although she had been told how she had made friends with the bold, bad man who afterwards robbed the bank at Northfield.

"Very soon afterward, at the age of 18, I believe, she became, as she had dreamed, in childhood, 'a newspaper man,' editing the St. Peter Journal, and to the hour of my pardon she was one of the most indefatigable workers for us.

"A few years ago failing health compelled her removal from Minnesota to Idaho, and Minnesota lost one of the brightest newspaper writers and staunchest friends that a man ever knew. Jim and I had a host of advocates during the latter years of our imprisonment, but none exceeded in devotion the young woman, who as a little tot had ridden unknowingly with the bandit who was soon to be exiled for life from all his kin and friends.

"Preliminary work on the Northfield robbery was got down to during the last week of August 1876, and while Pitts and I were waiting for Bob and Chadwell, who had gone up there to look over the ground, we scouted all over the country thereabouts and around Madelia in order to get ourselves familiar with the lay of the land. When the two boys joined us we divided into two parties and started for Northfield along different routes.

"On Monday night, September 4, the party I was with reached Le Sueur Center, where we had trouble finding places to sleep, as court was in session. Tuesday night we put on at Cordova, and Wednesday we were in Millersburg. At the same time Bob and his crowd rounded up in Cannon City, which was south of Northfield.

"On Thursday morning, September 7, we all came together on the Cannon River, on the outskirts of Northfield. That afternoon I took a look at the bank, and in camp at dinner I told the gang that no matter what came off we mustn't shoot anybody. While I was making this point as strong as I could one of the crowd asked what we should do if they began shooting at us. Bob at once said that if I was so particular about not having any shooting the best thing for me to do was to stay outside and take my chances.

"Well, at last the time came. Bob, Pitts and Howard started for town ahead, the scheme being that they should round up in the town square and not go into the bank until the rest of the party joined them. It was fixed that Miller and I should go on guard right at the bank, while the rest of the gang was to wait at the bridge and listen for a pistol shot signal in case they were wanted for help. We had it schemed out that as there were no saddle horses around anywhere we could get off with a flying start and get away before they could stop us, wrecking the telegraph office if necessary to prevent any alarm being sent out by wire.

"Whisky spoiled the whole plan. Between the time they left camp and reached the bridge the men who went ahead got away with a quart of whisky—the first time I had ever known Bob to drink, and as a matter of fact, I didn't know he had done so then until the day and its terrible events were over. The blunder was that when these three men saw us coming, instead of waiting for us to get up with them they slammed right on into the bank regardless, leaving the door open in their excitement.

"I was out in the street, pretending I was having trouble with my saddle. Meantime I had told Miller to close up the bank door. A man named Allen, who kept a store near by, was then trying to get into the bank, but Miller foolishly shouted at him and told him to get away. Allen at once became excited and saw that something was wrong, and ran off up the street shouting to every one to get his gun, as the bank was being robbed.

"A Dr. Wheeler, who saw that something was happening out of the ordinary, began to yell 'Robbery!' Then I saw we were in for it, and would need all the help we could get. I first called to Miller to come inside and get out of harm's way and then I fired a signal to the three men at the bridge for them to come up and help us, as we had been trapped.

"Chadwell, Woods and Jim came galloping up, and at the same moment that they arrived I heard a shot fired inside the bank. The three boys were firing their guns as they rode along, shouting to everybody they saw to get out of the way and get indoors, but I am quite sure they never killed anybody. My theory always has been that the man Gustafson, who was shot down in the street, was struck by a glancing shot from some of the citizens' rifles, as they were out blazing away at this time.

"Miller was then shot by a man named Stacy and his face filled full of bird shot. A man named Manning killed Pitts' horse, and, as a matter of fact, the street was full of flying lead, coming from every direction. It wasn't long before I was wounded in the thigh by Manning, and the next instant he shot Chadwell through the heart.

"Dr. Wheeler, from an upper floor of a hotel, got a bead on Miller and brought him down, so that he soon lay dying in the middle of the street. Every time I saw a man pointing a gun at me I dropped off my horse and tried to drive the shooter under cover, but there were so many of them, and I couldn't see in every direction, so I soon found out that, wounded as I was, I was helpless. Meanwhile there was a tragedy going on inside the bank.

"Bob came out in a hurry and started down the street toward Manning, who ran into a store; hoping he would get a shot at Bob from under cover. Bob ran on, but didn't notice Dr. Wheeler, who was upstairs in the hotel, behind him, and Wheeler's third shot smashed Bob's right arm. Bob switched his gun to his left and got on Miller's horse, thinking that Miller was dead. By this time Howard and Pitts had got out of the bank, and I told them that Miller was still alive and we'd have to save him. I told Pitts to put Miller on my horse, but when we lifted him I saw he was dead, so I told Pitts that I would hold off the crowd while he got away, as his horse had been killed. While Pitts ran, less than ten yards, I stood with my pistol pointed at anyone who showed his head, and then I galloped off and overtook him and took him up behind me.

"Pitts then confessed to me about the drinking, and said they had made an awful mess of it inside the bank. It had been arranged that they should hold up Joseph L. Heywood, the acting cashier, at his window, and after roping him get to the safe without any trouble. Instead of that, these three drink-crazed lunatics leaped over the rail and scared Heywood so badly that he immediately got on the defensive, and in a minute the alarm was out and it was all over.

"It seems that one of the robbers had waved his revolver at Heywood the minute he entered the bank and asked him if he was the cashier. Heywood had said he wasn't, and then the same question was put to the other two men who were in the bank. Each of the three said he was not the cashier, but the robber turned to Heywood, who was sitting at the cashier's desk, and said:

"'You're the cashier; open that safe d—n quick or I'll blow your head off.'

"Heywood jumped back and Pitts ran to the vault and got inside. Heywood then tried to shut him in, and was seized by the robbers, who told him to open the safe at once or he would not live another minute. Heywood told him there was a time lock on it that positively couldn't be opened, whereupon Howard pulled a knife and tried to cut Heywood's throat, the cashier having been thrown to the ground in the scuffle that had taken place. Incidentally, Pitts told me afterwards that Howard fired a pistol near Heywood's head, but only with the intention of frightening him.

"A. E. Bunker, the teller, by this time had tried to get hold of a pistol that was near where he was, but Pitts got the gun first, and it was found on him after he was killed, and consequently furnished just that much good evidence that we were the men at Northfield.

"The boys saw by this time that the safe could not be reached, so they asked Bunker about the money that was outside. Bunker pointed to a little tray full of small coins, and while Bob was putting them away in a sack Bunker made a dash through a rear window. Pitts fired at him twice, his second bullet going through his right shoulder.

"By this time the men in the bank had heard the commotion and firing outside and started to leave.

"Heywood, who had been on the floor, unfortunately rose at this instant, and Pitts, still under the influence of liquor, shot him through the head and killed him.

"Meantime we who had escaped slaughter in the terrible bombardment we had faced were trying to make our way to some safe place. Not far from Northfield we met a farmer, who lent us a horse for Pitts to ride, and we got past Dundas ahead of the news of the raid on the bank. We were also beating it at Millersburg, but at Shieldsville we ran into a squad of men who knew what had happened and were after us. These men had, foolishly for themselves, left their guns outside a house, and we didn't let them get hold of them until we had a good start, but they overtook us about four miles away and shots were exchanged without any trouble resulting.

"Soon there were a thousand men on our trail and about $5,000 in rewards for our capture. We tramped and camped and rode and watched in a strange country and among the lakes. We didn't know the trails and were afraid to try the fords and bridges, knowing that our hunters would be sure to keep their eyes on these places. Saturday morning we abandoned our horses and decided to keep up the fight afoot. We tramped all night and put in Sunday near Marysburg. Bob's elbow by this time was in pretty bad shape and we had to go slow. Finally, on Monday night and Tuesday we couldn't go anywhere, so we passed the time in a deserted house near Mankato. A man named Dunning found us there and we took him prisoner. On the theory that the dead are silent, some of the men wanted to kill him, but I wouldn't stand for that, so we made him swear by all that was holy that he wouldn't tell that he had seen us until we got away. Then we turned him loose. He lost no time in getting into Mankato and giving the alarm, and in a few minutes another posse was after us.

"That night Howard and Wood decided that they wouldn't hold back any longer and that we were losing valuable time because of Bob's wound, so they left us and went on west. They stole two horses very soon, and this helped us as well as them, for the posse followed the trail of the stolen horses, not knowing that we had divided.

"On Thursday morning, September 21, just two weeks after the raid, the end came. A party of forty men soon surrounded us and opened fire. We were cut off from our horses and our case was hopeless. We were on the open prairie and not ready for our last fight against such odds, we fell back into the Watonwan river bottom and hid in some bushes.

"When the iron doors shut behind us at the Stillwater prison we all submitted to the prison discipline with the same unquestioning obedience that I had exacted during my military service. The result was that we gained friends both in prison and outside. We had been in prison a little over seven years, when, on January 25, 1884, the main building was destroyed by fire at night. George F. Dodd was then connected with the prison, while his wife was matron. There was danger of a panic and a terrible disaster. Dodd released Jim and Bob and myself. To me he gave a revolver. Jim had an axe handle and Bob a small iron bar. We stood guard over the women prisoners, marched them from the danger of the fire, and the prison authorities were kind enough to say that had it not been for us there must have been a tremendous loss of life.

"I can say without fear of contradiction that had it been in our minds to do so we could have escaped from the prison that night, but we had determined to pay the penalty that had been exacted, and if we were ever to return to liberty it would be with the consent and approval of the authorities and the public. A little later Jim was put in charge of the mail and library of the prison, while I was made head nurse in the hospital, where I remained until the day we were paroled.

"As the years went by the popular feeling against us not only subsided, but our absolute obedience to the minutest detail of the prison discipline won us the consideration, and I might even say, the esteem of the prison officials. In the meantime it had been a life sentence for Bob, he having died of consumption September 16, 1889.

"Jim and I went out into the world July 14, 1901, after serving a few months less than twenty-five years. Each of us immediately found work, and life again took on its normal hues. Poor Jim, however, was subject to periodical spells of deep depression. The bullet that shattered his upper jaw in our last fight in Madelia imbedded itself near the brain and was not removed until long after we were in the prison at Stillwater. That bullet was the cause of his occasional gloominess. After our release from prison Jim's health continued precarious. He finally gave up the fight, and on October 19, 1902, took his own life in a hotel in Minnesota.

"I am not exactly a dead man, but I have been shot twenty-eight times and am now carrying in my body fourteen bullets that physicians have been unable to extract. Twelve of these wounds I received while wearing the gray, and I have ever been proud of them, and it has been one of my keenest regrets that I did not receive the rest of them during the war with Spain."

The following is an authentic copy of Cole Younger's commitment papers.

THOMAS COLEMAN YOUNGER

RICE COUNTY DISTRICT COURT
Crime: Murder 1st deg., '87
Term: Life. Sentenced Nov. 20, 1876.
Nativity: Missouri.
Age: 32 years.
Height: 5' 11 1/4"
Hair: Very light brown, very curly, thin and bald on crown of head.
Eyes: Blue (light).
Complexion: Fair, inclined to be florid.
Occupation: None.
Marks: Two moles on back; scar on left shoulder and small scar on left hip caused by gunshot.
Can read and write — uses tobacco — single — temperate.

RECORD
Removed to Washington County Jail, Jan. 26, 1884.
Paroled July 14, 1901.
Pardoned Feb. 4, 1903, on condition that he leave State of Minnesota and that he never exhibit himself in public in any way.

Editor's Note: It is surmised the names Howard and Wood indicate Jesse and Frank James respectively.

My First Train Robbery

BY GEORGE SONTAG

From *A Pardoned Lifer: Life of George Sontag, Former Member, Notorious Evans-Sontag Gang, Train Robbers,* written by Opie L. Warner (San Bernadino, California: The Index Print, 1901).

This tale he recounted to me—the apparently free life he had led, the train robberies, the money he had secured from them, which appeared with but little effort, the easy manner in which he eluded capture; left a mighty deep impression upon me. After he had gone, I spent many hours thinking of what he had told me.

Later, when he asked me to assist in holding up a train, he had to use no persuasion, for I had made up my mind that I would do so alone, if I could make arrangements.

John stayed at home only a short time, going back to California.

He had been back but a little while when he and Evans held up a train at Ceres. Their effort was not a success, as they were unable to get into the car.

Following this attempt John returned home. He had hardly been there a couple of days when he began to ask me about the trains in that section of the country. As I had spent many wears in braking, I was in a position to give him some valuable information.

I told him particularly of a train, No. 3, thinking that he was gathering data for a robbery for himself and partner.

One day, however, he said: "George, let's take the folks up to Chicago, and leave them there, while we hold up that No. 3 train."

As I said, it did not take any coaxing to get me to go into a deal with him, so we took the folks up to the "Windy City," with the purpose of holding up that train.

Train No. 3 ran out of Chicago, leaving there at 11 p.m. After going over the ground, we found that we could not ride her out of the Union station, so I took a trip down the line one night, and discovered that we could stop the train at Western Union Junction. This being the only place we could intercept her, we decided to make Racine, Wisconsin, the base of operation, and accordingly we left for that city leaving the other members of the family in Chicago.

The night was in November, 1891, when we left Racine. It was dark and stormy, and as we made the trip afoot out of Racine our progress was slow. Indeed, we were about to give up the idea during a lull in the storm, fearing that we could not successfully bring the deal off. Finally we concluded to stick it out. The fact that it was the first snow of the winter, when we, with everyone else, was caught unawares, made the deed more hazardous, and we were more than ordinarily cautious.

The train came in at the Western Union, on time, and we boarded it. When out where we thought we had decided was the right place, we "stuck her up."

However, we ran one crossing too far, a fact that put the train in closer touch with the officials.

We were some time in getting into the car. We both had covered the engine crew and made them get out of the cab to assist us in getting into the car. The messengers would not open up, so we went to work to blow off the doors. After firing three charges of dynamite the messengers, two of them, came out and delivered up the keys.

I went into the car, and told one of the messengers whom I took with me, to open the safe. He said: "Sorry; no coin tonight."

I stepped back and, cocking both barrels of my gun, told him to dig up. He said: "For God's sake, boy, don't shoot; I'll get it." He dug between some boxes where the money had been hidden. I made a search of the car and found three small safes. The messenger told me they were time locks, and could not be opened. I told him to get them out, as we could open any kind of a safe. They were too heavy, so I threw in a stick of dynamite and blew the safes out of the car, badly damaging the latter.

John started with the bunch for the engine, I hollering to him to wait while I blew the safes open. He answered back:

"Here comes a special from Racine." Racine was only seven miles away.

We took what money we had secured from the first "dig," $9,800, and left the scene.

The road was slushy, and we had a hard time getting to a cabin where we could break our guns and put them in their cases. We then proceeded to town. Arriving there we went home, our mother sleeping through the night and never dreaming that the sensation she saw in the papers next morning was caused by her two sons.

We learned that the safes that we blew out of the car contained $110,000, which, had we timed our stop more correctly, we could have secured.

The crossing at which we stopped afforded an opportunity for the train crew to get word to Racine.

After we left the train and broke our guns, we kept to the track, as we knew that the posse would come on a train, and we could step aside if we saw the special.

The train went on to Milwaukee, after we told the engineer to pull out.

Part Two

Convicts on Convicts

NOT MANY CRIMINALS have considered prison life con-
ducive to the enrichment of the soul. The few who have
transcended their surroundings have found an inner peace and
higher calling resulting from their confinement. The majority
of convict commentaries on their fellow colleagues are replete
with criticisms on the ill effects of prison life and on the concept of prison as a "school for crime." We encounter this view
of the prison as a den of iniquity instead of a place for penance
and rehabilitation right from the beginning of the penitentiary
system in the late eighteenth century. W.A. Coffey, for example, writing in the first quarter of the nineteenth century in his
memoir *Inside Out*, deplores the low state of convict morality.
He damns the convicts for their depravity, vices, and dissolu-
tion. He then goes on to criticize the low level of education
among convicts. To him, prison is only good for learning the
"science of iniquity." Coffey, a lawyer, offers the solution of
labor in complete solitude.

Coffey does not mention the prison of his woes, but it was
most likely Auburn in upstate New York. Auburn represented
one of the two leading schools of penology in the first half of
the nineteenth century. The Auburn system featured congregate labor in silence with solitary cells at night. The other system, that of the Eastern Penitentiary in Philadelphia, opened
in 1829, featured total solitary confinement and hard labor, as
recommended by Coffey. The two systems were the subject of

much debate among prison reformers of the period. But what Mr. Coffey didn't know, and others soon found out, was that lengthy solitary confinement usually induced insanity rather than penance. The Auburn system won out, but not because of any sympathy for the mental health of the convicts. Pure and simple, the Auburn model penitentiary was less expensive to build, and its congregate labor system and factories resulted in higher productivity in the prison and higher profits for the state. The Philadelphia-style solitary in-cell labor system limited the type of work a convict could do, and hence the costs of confinement were too high for the state to bear. But Coffey's criticisms reflect the spirit of the antebellum prison reform debate that raged among the advocates of the two systems.

William Stuart, writing in 1854, did not criticize or blame the prison system for its lack of reformative elements. His rehabilitation came from within when he decided that a life of crime was not for him. But until then he led the life of a rogue and rascal, and his descriptions of his adventures are some of the most amusing of the genre. After describing some of his adventures, he discusses the largely mythical thieves' code of honor. To be sure, many convicts do subscribe to the code. But we can say generally that if code is followed at all, it is mostly through fear of being branded and perhaps harmed as an informer. But Stuart's claim of being true to the precepts of his "secret society" of the underworld lends force to the public's perception of honor among thieves.

By the time Flave Weaver was writing shortly after the Civil War, most people rightly considered prisons as places of harsh punishment, hard labor, and profits for the state. Weaver found himself in the Kansas Penitentiary and working in that state's coal mines. The last lines of his selection remind us of the dreadful conditions prevalent in nineteenth-century prisons, when he moans, "My heart leaped into my throat as I thought of toiling day after day in the dark hole nearly eight hundred feet below the surface of the ground."

A few prisoners did find spiritual solace in prison, which led them to find a better life or higher calling. Jerry McCauley was one of those fortunate individuals. Arrested for robbery still as a teenager, the state sentenced him to fifteen years at hard labor. He used the cell to his advantage and found religion. After his release, McCauley founded a mission in New York City which is still operating today.

The convicted criminal not only has to survive *in* prison but also faces hardship, scorn, and difficulties upon release. Not many businesses want to hire an ex-con, either in the nineteenth century or later. D.B. Smith spent two years in the Iowa Penitentiary and strongly criticized the contract labor system then prevalent in the prison system. But he found that life was not that much easier upon release. Ill-trained and wearing the badge of pariah, he had difficulty finding work. The ex-convict then fell back on what he knew best: crime. The cycle continued, yesterday as today.

Franklin Carr's memoir is good evidence of this vicious circle. Carr kept returning to his life of crime and gambling and just as quickly made it back into the penitentiary. Number 1500 describes his stay in the Tombs jail in New York and then going "up the river" to Sing Sing (where the expression comes from, as Sing Sing lies on the banks of the Hudson River north of New York City), giving a lively description of the types of criminals he encountered there.

A Thief's Code of Honor

BY WILLIAM STUART

From *Sketches of the Life of William Stuart, the First and Most Cele-brated Counterfeiter of Connecticut; Comprising Startling Details of Daring Feats Performed by Himself—Perils by Sea and Land—Frequent Arrests and Imprisonment—Blowing Out of Jail with Powder—Failure of Escape After he Had Led his Cowardly Associates Out of the Horrible Pit, in Simsbury, into the Prison Yard, etc* by William Stuart (Bridge-port, Connecticut: Printed and Published for the Author, 1854).

I hired a black man to put me across the river, and I entered the forests, which in those days covered almost the whole country. The weather was warm, and I took a nap upon the leaves. When day-light appeared I bent my course to the N.E., and before night arrived at Coosahatchie, a village on the river of the same name. A widow woman kept tavern in the place, and I stopped for refreshments and rest. A neighbor of her's soon came into the barroom and wanted to borrow money of her, but she declined to lend him. This man became furious be-cause of her denial, and abused the woman in the vilest terms. I saw that she was becoming afraid of him, so I told him that I should not take part in the quarrel, nevertheless I should not sit by any longer and permit him to revile her. He looked at me with disdain and contempt, and commenced his tirade upon me, and I took him by the collar and put him into the street, then went back and closed the door. The woman thanked me for the service I had rendered her, and offered to keep me as long as I would stay, without charge. Having had a hard time on board of our ship, I gratefully accepted her offer, and tar-ried with her, as Paul said, "for the space of many days."

She was blessed by nature with genius adequate to any emergency, and her features were unrivalled by the choicest specimens of statuary; her tresses, black as the raven's wing, descended gracefully from her head; her eyes were black and lustrous as an houri's; her face seemed wrought with exquisite beauty; and her form was chaste and finely modeled. Her age about thirty, with all the charms of eighteen years, while a little daughter, fatherless, looked to her for support and protection. When I became more acquainted with her, I found that she, like myself, was hardened by fraud, dishonesty and corruption.

She kept her house open during the greatest part of every night, and when the outer world was clothed in darkness, the slaves from the neighboring plantations brought her corn, fowls and pigs, and articles of merchandise, for which she scantily paid them in gewgaws and whisky. She was ripe for almost every enterprise, and was willing to engage in any object that promised a golden reward. As our acquaintance became more thorough, I oftentimes recapitulated my pursuits, told her the stories of my life and the escapes that fortune had cast in my way, and the stratagems to which I had had recourse in my eventful history. I gave her an outline of my counterfeiting process, and she entered into my plan with her whole heart. She gave me access to all her business, and reposed confidence in my ability to do all things well. She denied me nothing, but was eager to anticipate my wishes for the pleasure of obliging me. When the subject of counterfeit money was discussed, her anxiety to procure it banished almost every other thought from her mind, and she was willing to part with me for a season on no other terms than that I should obtain a large amount of funds, subject to her disposal. After staying at her house for three months, I agreed to go north, visit my friends, proceed to the Canadian mint, gather some thousands, and return. She procured me genuine notes of the Savannah and Augusta banks as specimens for the engravers, and all things were in readiness for my absence during a month. I need not dwell on the parting scene though destined to be brief. It was accompanied with tearful eyes and throbbing heart.

I took my course for Charleston, and when in that city got a passage to New York on my way to Connecticut. At home I passed a few days, looked over my farm, called upon old associates, and laid plans for the future. I kept all my own special secrets. I never was guided by plans as advised in our conclaves, but adopted expedients as the time and circumstances indicated at the period of their occurrence.

Eliphalet Bennett and I started on foot for Canada together. He was a great genius in the way of wickedness, and the most heartless and graceless villain that I ever knew. His parents took great care in his having a thorough education. He passed through college and received its literary honors, engaged in the study of the law under the tuition of an able counsellor, and for a time promised to be an honor to his family and his profession. But he was a deeply wicked man, unmoved by affection or kindness, and though married early to an amiable lady, the connexion was only productive of misery. He set fire to his house because his wife, contrary to his will, attended Methodist meetings, and was arrested and put in jail, but his wealth and friends saved him from punishment. He drank deeply, and seemed to delight in crimes of the greatest magnitude and of the most horrid depravity.

This man went with me after funds. When we got into the bounds of Vermont he frequently preached to the Methodist brethren, and usually closed his services in appeals to their liberality. He stated to his audiences that while away upon his circuit, his house and all that it contained was burnt, and that he was on his way to a rich brother in Canada for aid, and that the smallest sums that they could spare would avail him much. We collected money for him, and he borrowed an over-coat of one, and many garments of others, promising to return them when he came back. Thus we worked our way to Canada.

I left Bennett on the frontiers and went to my old friends, produced my specimen notes, and in a fortnight returned home with $40,000 in my belt. In latter days I had learned to take the by-paths, to save trouble and hindrance; said but little, and avoided respectable public houses. This purchase had exhausted all my means, and my family was poor, unless I made a saving in disposing of my counterfeit funds.

I now stowed my money in my favorite hiding places near home, and stayed a few weeks to prepare my household to live through the winter, while I was away in Georgia. My intentions were kept by me in perfect secrecy. No man was able to divine my purposes or even conjecture concerning them.

After a few weeks it was necessary that I should go to Cross River, in Putnam County, NY, to transact some business, and on my way went through Ridgefield, and having lost my handkerchief, I stepped into the store of Abner Gilbert and bought one for one dollar, and by accident let his clerk have a bad five dollar note. I passed on eight or nine miles, stopped at a tavern at evening, and it was reported that a man dressed in short clothes had passed it. I tarried a little while, then left the house and went across the fields into a barn. This was empty and no place to rest. I now went out and gazed over the country, and spied a light in a house upon an eminence, and drew near to it, asked admittance and was received to their fireside. Soon I went to bed and was getting sleepy, when several men entered and inquired for me. As these men entered my room, I aroused from my slumbers and was about to jump through the window, but they seized me and I became quiet. While they were about the room, I slipped 2 five dollar notes under the bed-post, and have not learnt up to this day that they were ever found. They escorted me to Ridgefield the same night and put keepers over me, and I passed the night with my hands tied behind me. Next morning I offered Gilbert one hundred dollars to let me go, and his wife begged of him with tears in her eyes, but he was determined that my career should be checked.

Next day came on my trial, and I was sent to Danbury jail until the session of the court. I told the jailer that I had got home again, and he gave me some rum and I went into my room. My prospects were fair for Newgate but I cared very little about it. I was aware of the looseness of the watch that was held over me. Six or eight times a day Mr. Crofut, the jailer, with the still and stealthy step of a cat, would approach the grief-hole and peak at me. He did not intend that I should see him; but nothing escaped my vision, and though my face was frequently averted while he was casting suspicious glances at me, yet he never caught me unawares in any of my movements. I did not try to disturb his peace as I did that of his predecessor. I was pacific as a spaniel, and was thus throwing a mist before his eyes for future purposes.

It was in the last of November, 1817, if I rightly recollect, when I re-entered this den of sinners. I now had full leisure to take a retrospect of my previous life, and upon a rigid examination, after casting aside all my prejudices, was disposed to give a verdict against myself. Others had done wrong, violated the law, trampled upon justice, and outraged the good sense of the community, and were still abroad, verily leeches upon the country. In an evil hour I had been snatched up, and was compelled to look through grated windows and hear the rattling bolts of iron doors, while others were still bleeding the people at every pore. I comforted myself with the reflection that their turn, even if delayed, would eventually come.

But here I was, with irons about my ankles and wrists, that my keepers had unceremoniously brought into my presence unasked, introduced me to them, and compelled me to accept them as my present associates. Though I scorned them, for the sake of politeness and courtesy, I informally received them to my embraces and shook hands with them, not cordially, but because there was a necessity in the case. I thought of my contract with the Georgia widow, but was in no condition now to return to her hospitable home and carry out our intentions. I did not so much as write her a letter, informing her of the disabilities under which I labored, nor to inform her that I had used due diligence to augment her interests in pecuniary matters. In all these things I was silent.

My stay in Danbury jail was about four weeks, and the evening before I was removed the jailor came in and searched me. I had all my implements for jail breaking about my person, and gave them all up to him and abandoned the project. Next day I was waited upon the sheriff to Fairfield. I was as cheerful as if I was going to a dance or a quilting frolic. They put me in the prison, infested as it had been in summer with bugs, fleas, and lice. It was now cold weather, and they did not annoy me. A short time thereafter my trial came on, and as the testimony against me was positive, the jury brought me in guilty. One of the witnesses swore falsely against me, but there was truth enough to convict a saint in the testimony of the others. I was sentenced to five years' hard labor in the state prison.

After the judge had sentenced me, I rose and asked his honor this question: "Suppose, sir," said I, "I die before my five years expire, shall I have to provide a substitute to serve out the remainder of my term? I hate to cheat the state; will you please inform me in these matters, for I am ignorant of the law?" The judge smiled, and told me that in case of death these things would not be required of me. I felt better after the sentence of the court, convinced that justice would be observed by my punishment.

While I lay in Danbury jail, the judges of the court, the lawyers, the state's attorney, and many wealthy gentlemen engaged in mercantile pursuits, called on me and urged me to reveal to them the names of my associates, assuring me that I should leave the jail in a month and enjoy my liberty. My doctrine ever had been, and now is, if a person enters a secret society, no matter what its objects may be, and solemnly swears to keep secret all its operations and movements, none but those who are ready for perjury will be guilty of treachery. I told these men that I was my own counterfeiter, and that no man was acquainted with my operations. They knew I lied, and I knew it; but before I would entrap others to secure myself, I would be hanged on the nearest tree. I always inculcated a spirit of honor and integrity among our members, and if one of us should fall a victim to violated law, his mouth should be hermetically sealed in reference to his associates. I could keep a secret without effort, because it was pleasing to me to do so. The public are not benefited by the confessions of a rascal, and his oath is worthless who accuses others to screen himself. Such men are obnoxious to the people, and whenever in after life they become witnesses in court, they are regarded by those who know them with scorn and contempt.

Convicts
By W.A. Coffey

From *Inside Out; or, An Interior View of the New York State Prison* by
W.A. Coffey (New York: James Costigan, 1823).

*Man is an imitative animal. From his cradle to his grave, he is
learning to do, what he sees others do.* —Jefferson

The convicts are, generally, very bad, wicked and ignorant
men; with all the feelings, passions and propensities of man,
in unfettered society. It was, perhaps, necessary to make this
premise, as there are many well-meaning persons in existence,
who, viewing crime through the full medium of ignorance, believe it to have the faculty, like the finger of Midas, of trans-
muting what it touches—of instantly changing a man into a
daemon. I have heard children, while passing through the
prison as visitors, with the utmost astonishment exclaim, as
they narrowly eyed the convicts, "Why, dear me, they all look
like men!" I have heard middle aged persons wondering that
they were not chained; and I once remember to have seen an
elderly gentlewoman run, precipitately, out of one of the
prison shops, because one of the convicts had merely moved
from his seat. We are, in matter and mind, the same identical
being; actuated by the same impulses, exerting the same en-
ergies, and endowed with the same faculties. It is only in the
peculiar manner of exerting those faculties, as directed, either
by our actual want or diversity of education, that we, essentially, differ. The precepts of morality graduate, greatly, according to the contraction or expansion of the human mind.
Thus, you see a man whose uncultivated mind, in his infantile
years, was familiar with scenes of depravity and wickedness,
viewing their subsequent repetition, with neither astonishment nor horror. To him, they are no novelties: he saw them in
his infancy, he is not disgusted with them, in his manhood. But
that cultivated and virtuous soul, whose vision is unaccus-
tomed to turpitude, and who is not restrained from the com-

mission of crime by the mere *fear* of punishment, shrinks from vice as from the death-breathing Siroc. The stigma—the odium—the degradation of vice, are more awfully present to his soul, and operate more powerfully upon it, than all the penal codes, from the days of Solon, up to the present time. Place that man in any situation of life, and some traces of his virtue will linger still around him. Like the gaudy sculpture of a fallen column, in the region of desolation, his worth will be perceptible through the very solitude which surrounds him. Vice creeps slowly upon the soul. In a *moment,* no man ever reaches its summit: *Nemo repente fuit turpissimus.* He becomes gradually wicked, if in his infancy, he is virtuous.

Confined together, and having continual opportunities of unrestricted conversation, it is natural that the convicts should consummate friendships with, and imbibe the principles of each other. However indignant, at first, a man may be, at the loathsome lispings of vice, when he is so situated that he cannot avoid hearing them, they *soon* lose their primal horror and very speedily become familiar. Once tolerable, the step to the embrace of vice becomes easy in the extreme. Young villians soon become old knaves. The elder instruct the younger in the science of iniquity—day after day they concert plans of future perfidy—and nightly, they discourse upon nothing but depravity. Murder becomes a trifle, when it is necessary to their purposes; and many convicts are within this prison who have not scrupled to commit it. Connections formed with dissolute, abandoned and desperate men—men, practised in dissimulation and blackened by crime—whose determination is the attainment of their *ends,* without compunction at the means—such connections are destructive of morality and virtue, and expose the mind to all that is detestable in turpitude. Innumerable instances might be adduced to verify the fact. Convicts who had, mutually, promised to become partners in iniquity, and who had concerted their plans before their liberation, have often been seen waiting for each other, in the very view of the prison, and departing, in company, to practice their villianny. Some have been detected in their nefarious attempts, almost before they were without the purlieus of the prison. One instance is known of a convict's being liberated, detected in a theft, indicted, tried, convicted, sentenced to a ten years imprisonment, and returned to the prison, *all in one day.* And many instances of *second* and *third,* and some few of fourth, fifth and sixth convictions, serve essentially to prove that the present system, from the very intermixing of the convicts, is rather *generative,* than destructive, of vice. Among the convicts, there are generally several very small boys, whose age would indicate the utter impossibility of a maturity of guilt. They are placed among men, more experienced in crime, who treat them as adults, and impart their feelings to them freely. It is a common thing to hear a boy who can scarcely reach the top of a man's pocket talk openly of divesting it of its valuable contents. And, indeed, one would be led to suppose that some attempt of the kind generally succeeds a liberation, from the circumstance of there being so many *second* comers, at present, confined, who are scarcely of full age.

◆◆◆

It is really wonderful to observe the general dearth of talent among the convicts. Among so many men as there are in this prison, gathered as it were, from the four winds of the heavens, one would suppose that some few of *exalted* literary acquirements might, invariably, be found. But, to the credit of education be it said, the convicts are, generally, ignorant and unlettered men. So unusual is it for a man, of any erudition, to be found among them, that when one actually appears, the tinkling of his fame is heard many years after his absence, even oftentimes proceeding, from the very lips of the Keepers. An acquaintance with "Webster's Spelling Book," and with Arithmetic as far as the "Single Rule of Three," constitutes (with even many of the enlightened Keepers) a convict, a good scholar. I remember a fellow whose mere etymological parsing, obtained for him, a celebrity among the Keepers as well as the convicts, as extensive as that which the Colossus of literature enjoyed, during his valuable life time, in the republic of letters. He had a little smattering of English Etymology, which gave him the reputation of being an eminent grammarian; but he knew as much about Syntactical parsing as the most enlightened monkey in the island of Borneo. He was, however, the critic of the prison. Keepers submitted to him their literary disputes, and incredulity was hushed into immediate satisfaction by the reason and justness and infallibility of his decisions. Some, confidentially, communicated to him their conscientious scruples, and his casuistry, immediately, put pyrrhonism at rest. A line from his pen to the friends of a convict, in the estimation both of Keeper and of convict, like the querimonious notes of Orpheus, would draw tears from the very stones. Nothing was perfect in the *literary* world of the prison unless it received a wonder-working finish from his well acknowledged talents. He could draw a petition for a would-be-appointed Keeper, or fit a gold ring to his finger, with as much exactness and approved precision as nicety might require, or curiosity might wish. He worked at whitesmithing, and almost every other trade practised in the prison; and performed a thousand things, that none but an uncommon genius, like himself, would be capable of, or would be allowed to attempt. Was there any thing to be done nicely, he must be consulted about it; and generally in the sequel, it was committed to his skill. Like the Parish Clerk in the Review, he was

"Painter, Glazier, *Whitesmith here*
"In short, he was, *factotem.*"

My First Crime

BY FLAVE J. WEAVER

From *Six Years in Bondage and Freedom at Last: A Tale of Prison Life* by Flave J. Weaver (Whitesboro, Texas: News Print, 1867).

Be Kind to a Man When He is Down

When a brother goes wrong,
And is lost midst the throng,
And is past by the good of the town,
Just lend him a hand,
And help him stand;
Be kind to the man when he is down.

Chorus

Forgive and forget,
For there's good in him yet,
Though he drinks his sorrow to drown,
Just lend him a hand,
And help him to stand;
Be kind to man when he is down.

As he lost friends and home,
A poor stranger to roam,
To be met with rebuff and frown
Just lend him a hand,
And help him stand;
Be kind to a man when he is down.

There is rejoicing above,
For a soul won by love,
And a bright star will shine in your crown,
For a hand that you lend
To a life most spent.
Be kind to a man when he is down.

I was not a criminal then. I had no notion of being one, but we broke the laws of the land, and fled to Nebraska where we were arrested and locked in the jail. Of course we did not like to be locked up, but we did not realize the serious offense that we had committed. The jail was a small building in one corner of the court yard. During the afternoon a small boy was playing near the jail, and we induced him to hand us an iron poker which he had, and with this we broke off the lock and walked out in the broad day light. This shows how insecure the jail was and how green we were. No one noticed us, however, but in conversation with some boys, were told that they kept a large bloodhound with which to trail prisoners, and we were afraid to try and escape, and sat around until we saw the sheriff coming. I went across the street and spoke to him. The oath he used when he recognized us would not look well in print but he did not hesitate to take us in charge again and make the fastenings as secure as he could. They were plenty secure enough, seeing that we had no desire to escape.

On July third we were taken out of the jail, shackled together, and started for the Kansas line where the sheriff from Cloud County was to meet us and take us to Concordia for trial. We arrived at the town of Hubble on the morning of the fourth of July. Here we waited all day for the sheriff to arrive to take us down into Kansas. There was no jail at Hubble and we sat most of the day in front of the hotel strapped together. Here we attracted a good deal of attention, for a prisoner in that peaceful little town was a rare visitor. We were taken from Hubble to Clyde in Cloud County and spent the day handcuffed in the hotel office, and on the same evening we were taken to Concordia and placed in the Concordia jail to await trial.

Why describe the trial? The witness stand, the jury box, the august judge, the broken-hearted father, and the grief-stricken mother and sister? Here the love and protection of a parent for a wayward boy was powerless, for he was in the iron hand of the law. I stood in the prisoner's box and heard the sentence from the lips of the judge. "Eighteen months at hard labor in the Kansas Penitentiary."

In bidding good bye to the boys at the jail, I showed a bravado spirit thinking the eighteen months would soon be past and I would soon be set free to pursue some useful and honorable occupation. I was handcuffed and shackled with my partner in crime and taken to Lansing, and as I walked up the stone steps and saw the high stone wall and large gray buildings and thought of the dungeons and the mines, my confidence left me and I felt my position—a boy, friendless and a criminal, Oh! the remorse that overshadowed me. I felt that I never could hold up my head again. Then for the first time came the full realization of the crime I had committed. The large iron doors opened and creaked a hoarse welcome as it swung on its hinges shutting me from the world, from mother, father and sister.

On arriving at the penitentiary, the first place a convict is taken is to the warden. At this time Captain Smith was warden. We were brought into his presence and our shackles and handcuffs removed. The door to our left was then opened and the Deputy Warden stepped in. The Deputy Warden is the executive officer of the institution. He issues the orders to the other prisoners, regulates their work and personally has the supervision over them. Upon his entrance he gruffly told us to "stand up." We did so, of course. Our measurements and descriptions were taken. We were shown how to march, with folded arms and with hands on the shoulders of the one in front, in the manner of convicts. We were next taken to the tailor department where the citizen's clothes were changed for a suit of stripes. I noticed that the bearing of all the officials toward the convicts was very gruff, harsh and almost insulting. The suit of stripes which I received was not a new suit but a second-hand one, well worn and patched, blackened and begrimmed with the dirt of the mines. This also is according to the institution, for nothing is left undone that will degrade, break the courage, and make the convict feel that he is disgraced and beneath the notice of honest men. After putting on my striped suit, I was conducted to what is called the north wing cell house and incarcerated in a cell of the regular size— four feet wide, eight feet long and seven feet high.

This was early in the evening and after hearing the lock click in the door of this cell I investigated the furniture. I found a little iron cot hanging to the side of the stone wall, a cane bottom chair, and in one corner was a little table on which was a Bible. I picked up the book and as soon as I had discovered what it was I threw it down for I had not yet learned that it was a chart to Heaven. I occasionally read it afterwards merely to pass away the time, but the truths took hold on me then.

The door of the cell was made of iron grating, and I next looked out to see what kind of a view I had from my cell. What I wanted to see most was a human face with a little trace of kindness or sympathy for me, and such as me, but there was not a soul in sight. Then a feeling of loneliness crept over me such as I believe no one ever feels who has not lost his liberty by breaking laws of his country. Oh! for my home, my father, mother and little sister. But I had disobeyed my parents by breaking the laws of my country. I had sown and now I must reap.

As I sat in the gathering gloom, a feeling of despondency came over me and I thought of the events of the four short weeks since I left home. The feeling of despondency turned to despair and desperation till my brain reeled. While in this condition, I heard the retiring bell ring and somehow it turned my thoughts homeward and I resolved to endure my confinement like a man. Just then the guard came along and in a very gruff voice said: "What are you doing here, young man?" I said: "I am here because I can't help it." "I'll put you in the dungeon." He told me I was to retire when that bell rang and I promised to retire at once and he left. He passed by in a few minutes, and, to all appearances, I was fast asleep, but in reality it was near morning before sleep came to my tired, restless eyes.

The rising bell awoke me the next morning and after dressing, the officer came along, unlocked the cell doors, and as he did so he handed me a piece of past-board with the printed rules of the prison thereon, with the remark to read them carefully and obey them. He said disobedience was punished by starvation and the dungeon. The cell house that I was in had forty-three cells in a tier and four tiers of cells. Each tier of cells was called a division. My division was number one. After the cell doors were all unlocked the officer cried, "First division front." Each convict with his hand on the cell door stepped out and fell in line. We were then marched silently to the dining hall which has a capacity of seven hundred. The prisoners are seated twenty in a row and sit with folded arms till all are seated, then the Deputy Warden taps the bell and they proceed to eat. It is needless to say that this dining room scene with seven hundred human beings, clean shaven and hair closely clipped, clad in their dirty striped clothes, was neither cheering nor inspiring. When the prisoners sit down to the table, there is a tin plate, knife and fork with iron handles, and a little tin plate of hash before him. Every morning during the six years I was in prison we had hash, bread and a tin cup of coffee for breakfast. The piece of bread they gave me was four inches wide, two inches thick, and about a foot long. The prisoners have ravenous appetites on account of the limited fare and their hard work. I took my piece of bread and tasted each end of it and not being exceedingly fond of hash I waited for my coffee to cool. Before there was time for this a bell tapped and I arose and passed out with the rest. The prison instructions were to hold up your hands if we wanted anything, and I held up my hand. An officer noticed me and asked what I wanted. I told him I wanted my breakfast and he replied: "That is all right, you can get it tomorrow morning."

I was then taken to factory number five where the iron work is done for the Caldwell Wagon Company. The officer turned me over to the Superintendent. He took me to the other end of the factory where a prisoner was standing beside an anvil and a furnace. The Superintendent said: "Did you ever use a sledge hammer, Weaver?" I told him I had not and he said, "to try it." I picked up a sledge and the other prisoner held a piece of iron on the anvil. I made up my mind to try and do my work right and I struck at the piece of iron but missed iron, anvil and all. He said, "try again," and I did so but struck too close to the prisoner's hand and he dropped the iron as if hurt. The Superintendent smiled and said, "try again," and I did so and that time struck the iron properly, and he said: "That is all right, you will make a blacksmith." I thought this was consolation. The Superintendent kindly informed us that we must weld eighty wagon tires per day or we did not eat. Our business was to weld tires, then take them to a round hole in the ground and drop them in. A large fire was then built in this hole and when the tires were sufficiently hot we would take a tire from the blazing hole with long iron tongs and take it and drop it on a wheel. Thus we worked week after week without speaking a word.

After working at the blacksmith trade for two months the Superintendent came around one day and said business was getting a little dull and they were going to send me to the coal mines the next day.

Oh! the dreaded coal mines; my heart leaped into my throat as I thought of toiling day after day in the dark hole nearly eight hundred feet below the surface of the ground.

Going to Prison

BY JERRY MCCAULEY

From *Transformed; or, The History of a River Thief, Briefly Told* by
Jerry McCauley (N.P.: Published by the Author, 1876).

> *"Oh, the darkness, how it thickens*
> *Like the brooding of despair!*
> *And my soul within me sickens —*
> *God, in mercy, hear my prayer!"*

I was only nineteen years of age when I was arrested for high-
way robbery — a child in years but a man in sin. I knew nothing
of the criminal act which was charged to my account; but the
rumsellers and the inhabitants of the Fourth ward hated me
for all my evil ways, and were glad to get rid of me. So they
swore the robbery on me, and I couldn't help myself. I had no
friends, no advocate at Court (it is a bad thing, sinners, not to
have an advocate at court), and without any just cause I was
sentenced to fifteen years in State prison. I burned with
vengeance; but what could I do? I was handcuffed and sent in
the cars to Sing-Sing

That ride was the saddest hour of my life. I looked back on
my whole past course, at all my hardships, my misery and sins,
and gladly would I have thrown myself out before the advanc-
ing train, and ended my life. It was not sorrow for sin that possessed me, but a heavy weight seemed to press me down when
I thought of the punishment I had got to suffer for my wrong-
doings, and an indignant, revengeful feeling for the injustice of
my sentence. Fifteen years of hard labor in a prison to look forward to, and all for a crime I was as innocent of as the babe
unborn. I knew I had done enough to condemn me, if it were
known; but others, as bad as I, were at liberty, and I was suffering the penalty for one who was at that hour roaming at will,
glorying in his lucky escape from punishment, and caring nothing for the unhappy dog who was bearing it in his stead. How
my heart swelled with rage, and then sank like lead, as I

thought of my helplessness in the hands of the law without a friend in the world.

I concluded, however, before I reached the end of that short journey, that my best way was to be obedient to prison rules, do the best I could under the circumstances, and trust that somebody would be raised up to help me.

When I arrived at the prison—I shall never forget it—the first thing that attracted my attention was the sentence over the door: "The way of transgressors is hard." Though I could not read very well, I managed to spell that out. It was a familiar sentence, which I had heard a great many times. All thieves and wicked people know it well, and they know, too, that it is out of the Bible. It is a well-worn proverb in all the haunts of vice, and one confirmed by daily experience. And how strange it is that, knowing so well that the way is hard, the transgressors will still go in it.

But God was more merciful to me than man. His pure eyes had seen all my sin, and yet he pitied and loved me, and stretched out his hand to save me. And his wonderful way of doing it was to shut me up in a cell within those heavy stone walls. There's many a one beside me who will have cause to thank God for ever and ever that he was shut up in a prison.

Problems After Release

By D.B. Smith

From *Two Years in the Slave-Pen of Iowa* by D.B. Smith (Kansas City, Missouri: H.N. Farrey & Co., 1885).

It is a prevalent belief among a large class of citizens, and on the face of it looks quite true, that there are certain men not satisfied outside of the penitentiary; and if you ask why, they will cite you to instances of men being in there two, three, four and five times; conclusively proving to their minds that these men regard the pen as their homes. Well, that looks very reasonable, and it is quite questionable if some of these men have not come to regard it as such. Well, such being the case, let us look around for a moment at some of the causes that have conduced to this result. A man is arrested for a crime, and no matter as to the general result about his guilt or innocence, if he has any money it will be all given either to lawyers or otherwise before he strikes the "pen." Well, he serves his time out, and if his own clothes are moth-eaten or lost, he is given a new suit, which, *capapie,* costs seven dollars, and the munificent sum of three dollars in money, also a railroad ticket to the place he came from. Now, if this man has not learned during his imprisonment some useful trade, and there is only about one out of every twenty that does, he is down to pretty close quarters. If he does not get work within a week, he is certainly out of money. Some one says, go to the next town; you will be apt to find work there. He goes and his circumstances follow him. He behaves himself, but can get no work; a policeman meanwhile has him spotted, and the daily paper next morning comes out with something like this: The ex-convict that is loafing around town here is watched, and had better make himself scarce. Now he picks up the paper somewhere and reads this. What shall he do? No use in looking for work here any longer; he is out of money; but he is scared and must go, so off he starts on a tramp. Maybe he will find work at some farm-house and maybe he will not; at any rate he must eat, and if he cannot obtain it one way he will another. Maybe he will find employment before nature compels him to steal, and maybe he will not. If the fates decide against him, back he goes to serve another term. Again, a man comes out of there and misses his train. There are always some fellows here who will take him in and do for him if allowed. They will take him to some saloon and get him drunk, if possible, and get all his money; so soon as that is accomplished he will be arrested for being drunk and disorderly, put in the city calaboose and fined, and committed twenty or so days and made to work it out, and now when he comes out he is all broke up; mad at himself, mad at everyone else, mad at the world in general, and is ripe for treason, strategem and spoils; and if he is caught in this condition by some designing person he falls, and back he goes.

Again, this class of men furnish rich and easy pickings for officers at times, and it is perfectly safe to take what they have under any circumstances, for they have no friends, usually, and no one to see that they are righted. An instance of this kind came under my observation during my sojourn in Madison, just before my going to the pen. They detained me some days at the jail before going up, and this incident occurred meanwhile. One day the marshall and deputy came in with an arrest. In this town the jail answers both for city and county purposes. The person under arrest was a fair looking young man, some twenty-five or more, had on very good clothes, a good overcoat, a watch and chain, and a nice valise in his hand; he had a scared look on his face, and my attention was almost immediately attracted toward them by his exclaiming, "Gentlemen, I don't deny that I am an ex-convict, but I am here on business and have done nothing wrong, neither is it my intention to; I am on my way home, and want to get there as soon as I can." Upon being questioned, he said he was working in Quincy, Ill., in a foundry; that a sick friend in Galesburg, same state, had written him twice to come and see him, urging that he was very sick, and wished very much to see him, that he finally quit work, bought his valise, put his clothes in, went up to see him, and he was now on his way home; had merely stopped off the train to see a friend with whom he had become acquainted during his imprisonment here. Well, the two marshals and the deputy sheriff searched him, took his valise, watch, pocket book and other traps, and threw him into the cooler to await further orders. They kept him there some three days, he all the time declaring that he had done nothing, and asking them to take him out before the mayor or squire, that he might be discharged and go about his business. Now the officers hunted around to find someone who, during this time, it is to be supposed, had seen him do something, but failed in their endeavors, and so they either had to turn him out free or prefer some sort of charge themselves; so one of them preferred the charge of drunk and disorderly, and Mayor Alley fined him one dollar and costs, and they brought him back to the jail. Now, what do you suppose they did? They asked him would he give up his things to pay his fine, or would he lay in jail and work it out, and he said, "Why, of course I must get home, and I will give up anything I have got to get out of here," and so they went to work and divided up his things. A nice seven-dollar valise and shawl-strap the deputy sheriff took; the watch a nice nickelplated one, worth probably twelve dollars or so, one of the marshals took, agreeing to pay the other so much, and pay the squire's dollar. There were also a few other little things of which I have now forgotten who took, and the poor fellow was let go without any thing but the clothes he had on, and he appeared glad enough to get away with them. Now, it was about three blocks from where he was arrested to the jail, and if he was drunk when he was arrested, he got sober quicker than any man ever did before in history, for he was certainly duly sober when he came in, and they came direct, as their conversation indicated. Now, if this was not a piece of bare-faced robbery perpetrated on this poor, helpless ex-convict, just because he was one, what was it? and this done by two marshals of the city and a county deputy sheriff, who afterwards became sheriff. Three principal officers in a county perpetrate a crime that Polk Wells would be ashamed to do at any time, and probably never did do so mean an action in the way of robbery. Now, if this poor wretch had to steal some money from some one before he got to work again and went to the "pen" again for it, who would be to blame, and would it show that he had rather be inside the "pen" than out of it?

No one can appreciate quite what these men have to contend with. In my own case, after coming out I asked a friend, or supposed friend, for a situation. He wanted some one and knew that I could perform the duty, and yet he said it would hardly do—he might lose the trade of Tom Brown or John Smith by my attending to the business—selfishness, you see, stepping immediately to the front, notwithstanding that prior to this time I had done this man more kindnesses than he will ever stop to count up either in this life or the next.

Well, so it is and so we appear to be constituted. Let your rod of censure then fall as lightly as possible on these poor unfortunates who appear to make the "pen" their home, for they are but poor, weak, frail humanity at best.

Gambler and Blackleg

By Franklin Carr

From *Twenty-Two Years in State Prisons* by Franklin Carr (Philadelphia: Gazette Printing Co., 1893).

We had on the second floor of a saloon a gambling room. I remember one old gentleman with long white hair, over eighty years of age, and who was worth considerable property. His poor old wife, who was aged and infirm, used to stand outside and cry and wring her hands, waiting for him to come out; but he never would go out till he had lost every dollar that he carried. I do not know what became of him afterwards. That is one of the many cases that I have seen ruined in the gambling saloon. A gambler is no more or less than a thief. He will rob you of every cent that you own. If he allows you to win ten or fifteen dollars he has a purpose for doing so; but if he thinks there is no more to be got from you he will not allow you to win anything. They will tell you that faro bank is the fairest game there is with cards, but there is a certain working of that little silver box whereby a professional gambler can draw out red or black card as he pleases. So you can see that you have not a ghost of a chance with a professional gambler. Most all gamblers I ever knew learned playing cards at home; just a social little game for pastime. Then they would play for pennies to make it interesting, and from that went to gambling for a living.

That was the first I got acquainted with gamblers and thieves. There was one in particular that I took a great fancy to. He was a great man in my eyes. They called him "Captain." He said he would make a good man out of me, and told me some great yarns that I would have plenty of good clothes, plenty of money and a good time of it, and when he took me away from there one evening he took me to a house in the lower section of the city where he said I would have a good time and the boys would like me; but when I got there that house fell in my estimation considerably. Instead of them liking me they got to fighting over me. It was a small square room with a small table in the middle of the floor, and a lot of men sitting around playing cards, and a girl sixteen or seventeen years of age filling up the glasses with liquor for them to drink. As we came through the door they jumped to their feet and wanted to know what he brought that boy there for, and they soon got to fighting with knives. As I saw the glimmer of the knives in the glare of the lamp I was very much frightened; boy-like, I shrank off in a corner for I was not so hardened in sin as I afterwards became. The captain told them to let me alone; I had the right stuff in me and I would make a good man. So the girl that was waiting on them got them quiet again, and one of them took hold of me by the collar and pointing a revolver in my face said he wanted me to listen to him; he said if I would ever "squeal" on them in any way he would shoot me like a dog. Then he told me to take my seat and offered me a glass of whiskey; I told him I did not want it. But he made me drink it, "for," he said, "you will want it before morning." About midnight one of them said, "Well, Jim, get the tools ready and let us get to work."

I wondered what kind of work they did at that hour of the night, but I was not kept long in ignorance. They brought the tools out and looked them over, and then they asked if he had the jimmy nipps, and if they had the lanterns and drills, and a number of other tools too numerous to mention. When they were ready they buttoned up my overcoat and wrapped a scarf around my neck and we were soon on our way out of the city on the cars. That was my first lesson in the art of a cracksman or a burglar.

We went into a small town up the State and were robbing a mansion, when some one coming home late gave the alarm. That was the first time I knew what it was to have a howling mob after us. A lot of farmers got after us with lanterns, shot guns and pitchforks; it was after a hard rain and the roads were full of mud. I ran till I was exhausted and covered with mud and could run no longer. I was so frightened I threw myself down by a fence in a corner and for some reason or other they passed me by and went after the men. The next morning when I got back into the city I was in a sorry plight, and had anybody taken an interest in me I believe it would have been my last step in crime; but I was left to myself and soon got as bad as the rest of them, so much so that I had to leave the city and go West. I went out into the State of Ohio where I got in with a gang of crooks as bad as any I had left behind in Philadelphia. There I changed my name and went under the name of Bill Pool. I now began to study the business as a profession, and was soon known as one of the worst in the State. I had joined a gang known as the "Bell Boys." There were three of them in the penitentiary at that time, and a woman who kept what is known among crooks as a "fence," furnished me with a set of burglars' tools, and I soon became a terror to that State. I had robbed a place up at McCoy station and then cut a boat loose on the river and rowed down to Steubenville. Then I set the boat adrift and took the steamboat Othello, on my way to Wheeling, West Virginia, to commit a crime, but before we got there the boat was hailed at Martin's Ferry where the authorities came aboard and put my partner (a young man by the name of John Hamilton) and me in irons. We were taken, by rail, back to Steubenville. I waived a hearing at the time so I could hear from my friend and get counsel. Two days after I was bound over in $2000 bail to appear at court, and when I came up for trial I was four days getting tried. The sheriff spoke a good word for me and said I had behaved like a gentleman while under his charge in the jail, and when the judge told me to stand up for sentence he said, "I could give you ten years, but your counsel has pleaded so earnestly, and the sheriff has spoken so well of you, that I will give you five years in the Ohio penitentiary where you will find that the way of the transgressor is hard."

It was announced in the papers that we would be taken to the penitentiary the next day, but we were not taken for two or three days after. When I got out of there I met the sheriff again, and he said he did not expect to get us there without a good deal of trouble, for he thought some of the gang would attack the train somewhere along the road, and that was the reason we did not go up as advertised.

When I got in that prison I did find that the way of the transgressor was hard. They took me into one of the cell-houses, and there we found a guard who told us to take a seat. I tried to speak to him, but he told me to keep my mouth shut until I was spoken to. Then he took a card from his desk about two feet long and about ten inches wide, and when he read it to me I found I was not to talk, laugh, wink, look at visitors or the other prisoners, or do anything but what I was told to do. I found that the least infringement of these rules brought a ducking in the tub until one was almost drowned. I was taken from the cell-house to the bath-room and put under the shower bath, and my own clothes taken away and a striped convict suit handed to me to put on. Then I was marched over to the chapel, which was called the idle room, where we had to sit in rows through the week, and were not allowed to speak a word to those alongside of us. There was a guard to watch us that we should not talk, and woe unto the one that was caught moving his lips.

◆◆◆

I now commenced my life as a gambler on the Mississippi river, making St. Louis my headquarters. We would gamble from St. Louis to Memphis, Cairo and New Orleans, and back again. I kept up this life for some time until I was run off the boat as a gambler and a blackleg, and as a nuisance generally. Then I went to gambling on the railroad, going up one road and down another until we were run off the railroads.

One day while walking out Carondelet avenue I met two friends who said they had a job up the State and wanted me to help them. We went up the State of Missouri about two hundred miles, and came very near never coming back again, for we were caught by a vigilance committee and narrowly escaped lynching. In fact, we would have been if it had not been for the sheriff who rescued us from mob law by gathering a posse of deputies. Then they put us in jail and placed a strong guard around us, not that they were afraid we would escape, but that they wanted to keep them from molesting us. When we were brought up in court the judge gave us five years in the Missouri

State Penitentiary. The prison was built upon a high bluff alongside of Jefferson City; and below the prison was the quarry.

Below that was the Missouri Pacific Railroad, along which the guards were stationed, armed with guns, to see that we did not escape. Below the railroad ran the Missouri river, the swiftest river in the world, which could carry a man ten or twelve miles down stream before he could reach the other side. I came to the conclusion that I would have to stay my time out at that prison. In addition to the force already mentioned, any citizen would arrest a convict who tried to escape, hunting him down with dogs and guns and he would be well nigh perished when brought back. When I entered the prison they asked me what I did for a living. I did not like to say I did nothing but steal, so I told them I was a bartender. They said I was just the man they wanted to tend bar. I did not know what they meant at the time, but the next day he put me in the quarry, and put a large iron crowbar in my hand, and told me to attend to that. Not being used to that kind of bar, I soon had my hands full of blisters.

When I got out of that prison I went away with the intention of doing better. I thought as I had not made a good citizen I would perhaps make a better soldier, so I went to Leavenworth, Kansas, and enlisted in the regular army. I was sent from there to Fort Larned, and I found that the devil was just as strong in the army as in citizen life, for I was in the guard house most of my time for being drunk and fighting. One day I went on a pass to a town seven miles and a half from the fort, and staying over my pass was put in the guard house for absence without leave. The next morning at guard mount, when the officer of the day called my name, I did not answer quickly enough to suit him, so he struck me with his sword and called me a name I would not take from any man at that time, and the consequence was I knocked him down for it, and was court martialed and sentenced to carry a thirty-six pound ball and a six foot chain riveted to the left ankle for three years. General Pope reduced the term to one year, and I carried that ball two months before court martialed and one year afterward. I had to work with it from sunrise to sunset, in the hot sun, and sleep with it all night; had to cut wood for the officers' quarters, and when they didn't want any wood cut I had to dig a hole and then turn around and fill it up again. After serving my term in the guard house (I was then in Fort Dodge with my company) I was discharged for disability.

I Go to Sing Sing

By Number 1500

From *Life in Sing Sing by Number 1500* (Indianapolis: The Bobbs-Merrill Co., 1904).

About noon, on the day succeeding my sentence, I was notified to make ready to go to Sing Sing.

It was not an entirely unpleasant summons. Little as I knew what was before me, I was confident that it could not be worse than the Tombs Prison where I had spent three months amid a crowd of noisy, foul-mouthed, cheap criminals of the kind that New York City breeds easily. Vermin swarmed in the cells, and the turnkeys, like the horse-leech, cried, "Give, give," until my small reserve of money was nearly exhausted. The turnkeys were a little cleaner than the majority of the prisoners, except in speech, and were more noisy. My cell-mate at this time was a gambler who had shot three men in a bar-room fight. He was a cheerful fellow, assured of the justice of his cause and confident that a righteous judge and an unbiased jury would give him his freedom; but with the suspicion of his class, born of a careful study of the nether side of human nature, he was fearful that neither on the bench nor in the jury box would he meet either one or the other. However, he broke away from the discussion of his own serious affairs to cheer me up with such hopeful things as he could think of. How hollow was all he said—but how helpful it was in that day of trial and fear!

"Why, you don't do ten years, you know; only about six, maybe less. Your time is commuted by good behavior, and of course it's up to you to behave the very best you know how. You'll get to work right away and employment will kill time. The days will be occupied and at night you'll be tired and sleep ten hours, maybe twelve. That's half your time. It's like coming out in three years; that's what you'll do, three years. You'll have books and if you can get a pack of cards you can play patience. There's nothing that eats up the black dog like patience— though possibly you can't get a pack of cards there. But don't worry; you won't have to work beyond your strength. The doctor will look out for your health, the chaplain for your soul; you won't have any rent to pay. Everything will be provided; you won't have a care. Say, you can't have a single worry. It will be paradise, if you only look at it right. That's what it'll be, paradise. Let's take a drink. I hear the sheriff outside rattling the handcuffs. How!"

Nothing was easier to get in the Tombs than dope and whisky. Food wasn't cheaper and my cell-mate had an abundant supply of good spirits. He made a couple of stout high-balls which we drank with satisfaction and then my summons came. There were seven convicted men in my group and we were handcuffed four and three together. One of my companions was an electrical engineer, a graduate of Stevens Institute, who was sentenced to four years for burglary. He figured in the newspapers as the "mysterious burglar," and the romantic school of reporters built him up a reputation that made Eugene Aram's history pale and insipid. As a matter of fact, he was a drunkard and when in his cups would wander off into office buildings or apartment houses and steal what he could, from a copper boiler to a watch, and sell it for drink. Nevertheless, was a man of good manners and personally clean.

A jaunty young thief, neatly dressed and making his fourth trip up the river, completed our trio. The other four men were middle-aged tramps with jail-bird written all over them. As soon as we were ironed we were marched off to the van which stood in the yard and pushed inside, the door was locked, leaving us in gloom, the driver cracked the whip and shouted to the gate-keeper that he was slow in getting that gate open, the wheels turned on the rough stone pavement drowning the voice of the jaunty young thief who was trying to sing, "I'm off for Sing Sing for fifteen years," and our journey began.

I had looked forward to this particular experience with dread and loathing. I had, at times, seen at the Grand Central Station a gang of handcuffed men, herded by sheriffs, being pushed through the eagerly curious crowd who stared at them and with unreserved comment, pointed out the notorious characters, and gave short histories of their criminal careers. I had even paused to gaze upon them myself, perhaps entertaining for a moment the terrible fancy that some day, I, too, might be in the station, and that a crowd would gaze at me with the morbid interest and unsympathetic regard I had bestowed upon others. That fear was now realized, and as the van drew near the station, I trembled with foreboding before the ordeal.

The van backed up at the waiting-room entrance and the door flew open. There was the crowd filling the sidewalk, the newsboys and boot-blacks crouched in the front rank, men and women pressing against each other and staring with cold, curious eyes upon our misery. I didn't hear what they said, but I knew what they were saying. Suddenly I saw a reporter perched in the window and leveling his camera upon us. I had a compact parcel of underclothing in my free hand and with an impulsive movement, I hurled it at the kodak with true aim, knocking it out of the reporters hand into the area below.

"Hi! hi!" yelled the crowd, delighted with this added excitement. "Good boy," cried a tall man, thrusting a bunch of cigars into my bosom. "Hit 'em again!" In the midst of this confusion, the sheriff hustled us into and through the waiting-room and on to the train platform, not yet opened for the other passengers. Seats were found for us in the smoking-car and the young thief took up his song about going to Sing Sing for fifteen years.

Somebody touched me on the shoulder. It was the tall man who had forced upon me the cigars.

"I liked that trick, old fellow. You've got spirit. You'll get through it all right. How long have you got?"

"No talking to the prisoners," growled the sheriff.

"That's all right, Doyle. He's an old friend of mine. Don't you know me? I'm one of the Pinks!"

"Oh, all right," replied Doyle, accepting the proffered cigar. "I didn't see it was you."

All the prisoners were smoking and exchanging confidences. I had enough of detectives and turned my head resolutely out of the window. The crowd was gathering on the platform. A woman stood near the window looking into my face. From where she stood she could see the steel bracelet and chain that linked me to the mysterious burglar. He saw it, too, and cast his handkerchief over the glistening chain. My eyes fell under her clear, pitying gaze and just then the train moved. I took one more glance and saw that her own were filled with tears. Then she leaned over and clasped to her bosom the boy of six or seven years of age. I knew what was in her heart. It was a prayer for her son that in his life he should meet no such a fate as mine. Then the tunnel engulfed us in darkness.

✦✦✦

Adams, the policy king, with his millions behind him, and his custom of good and gentle manners, accepted his lot as a prisoner with dignity and composure. He was a man of the world in the broadest sense, a student, by which is meant more than a mere reader of the best literature, a patron and lover of music, in which he was no mean performer, a judge and lover of art and, whatever else he was with reference to business and politics, a man of refined tastes and cultivated manners. No doubt he had fully counted on the possibilities of his career, and foresaw what might at almost any time befall him; so that when he came to prison he was in a great measure prepared for the ordeal. At all events, no prisoner that came to Sing Sing in my time accepted his lot with a more serene philosophy or had less complaint to make over the conditions in which he found himself.

In the exchanges I saw press reports of his reception and I also witnessed with my own eyes most of that ceremony. Nothing that was printed in the newspapers about it had more color of truth than was contained in the bare fact that he was admitted as a prisoner and that he put on convict dress. One paper described the prison uniform he wore in detail, mentioning that it was a second-hand suit and a misfit for him, the trousers baggy at the knees, patched at the seat, and fringed at the bottom. As a matter of fact, he was received in the state shop and carefully fitted with a new suit that was altered to his measure on the hour of his arrival. Its cutter was a convict, but had designed clothing for men who were as punctilious in their dress as Adams could have been; and although the pattern of the cloth was against him, Mr. Adams put on a suit that fitted him quite as well, although it wasn't so becoming as the one he laid aside. On his first night he slept in a cell, but it was a clean cell with new bedding direct from the hospital. The next day he went into the hospital, where he remained during his term of imprisonment, coming out of it only for an hour's exercise daily in the yard in good weather. The patient in the prison hospital has nothing to envy in the condition of any hospital patient elsewhere who may be paying twenty-five or thirty dollars a week. The medical officer, Doctor R.T. Irvine, is a man of the very highest professional attainment, a surgeon of acknowledged skill and accorded reputation, so that professional treatment of the best kind is assured. The equipment of the hospital includes trained nurses and capable servants, and in furniture and arrangement embraces many comforts. It is, however, part of the prison; its windows are barred, a uniformed keeper has charge of its discipline; but the rules for the patients are few and mild and in fact far less rigid than those enforced in many of the hospitals in New York City.

So that, aside from the fact that Adams was a prisoner and had to wear the distinctive dress, he underwent no physical suffering. His diet was, of course, not what he had been accustomed to have, substantial, abundant, and if not daintily served, was clean and inviting. It included good milk, fresh eggs, butter, oat meal, soup with a joint or fish for dinner, tea and coffee with vegetables, and preserved fruits or puddings for dessert. That was the dietary scale and he could add to it very much what he wished by purchase from the village market. But it must be remembered that all of these luxuries and many more, as long as they do not include liberty, are only an amelioration of little hardships—not an improvement of condition. It doesn't matter what you do for a prisoner—so long as you do not release him from bondage, you haven't done anything. And on the contrary, any punishment you inflict upon him after he has experienced the lock-step can not greatly signify; for in that one act you have inflicted the punishment beside which all others are only trifles. For this reason men do not mind severe discipline nor appreciate mild treatment. Of course they can be dealt with so as to be irritated beyond endurance, but only by spasmodic and uncertain authority. A rigid control is met half-way, and with indifference.

Adams spent most of his time reading or chatting with his mates. There was nothing "stuck up" in his treatment of the convicts. He was genial and pleasant, helping many who applied to him for advice or assistance, and taking an interest in the little affairs of the prison. He read Dante, Pope's translation of Homer, Grote's *History of Greece,* Shakespeare, occasionally a new novel; but for lighter hours found in Dumas' *Count of Monte Cristo* and other works of the same vivacious author entertainment and pleasure. Altogether he was a model prisoner. His age and infirmities made it reasonable that he should have special treatment and perhaps there were other agencies whose potency is as active in prison as elsewhere.

Bissert, the police detective, didn't stay in Sing Sing long, but he had no such easy time as Adams. It would have been rather difficult to make it easy for Bissert. He was known and despised by every convict from New York City and they would have made effort to secure publicity of any favoritism that might have been shown him, and they would doubtless have succeeded. Besides that, there could be no excuse for relieving Bissert from the ordinary routine of work. He was a big husky fellow who knew a trade and had worked at it, and was in good physical condition and had no fine sensibilities to be outraged. Like all men who have the streak of yellow in them, he whined under the discipline and over the little bit of work required of him in the mat-shop; particularly he complained about the danger he was exposed to by association with convicts. This plea was not without some grounds. These same convicts had been exposed to real dangers at his hands, and his methods of securing conviction had been in several cases of a kind to invite reprisal. There was one man, Duncan Young, a life prisoner who was sentenced upon Bissert's testimony, who claimed to be innocent and the victim of the policeman's perjury. He had sworn to revenge himself and was a man to carry out his threats; but fortunately for Bissert when he came within Young's reach in prison, the latter was expecting a new trial, from which he could reasonably look for his freedom, but whose favorable prospects would be ruined by avenging his wrongs on Bissert. He got his trial, was reconvicted and resentenced to life; and when he returned, Bissert had obtained his release from Sing Sing on a writ.

The case of Young furnishes an illustration of the law's uncertainties. In his first trial for murder, the charge was sustained by Bissert's testimony. On his second trial, the police dug up the body of the man he was charged with shooting and took therefrom the fatal bullet, which corresponded with the pistol they swore was taken from Young with one barrel recently discharged at the time of his arrest. Young, on his second return to prison, got a third trial on a second appeal in which he offered evidence to show that he never had a pistol at all and certainly none at the time he was charged with killing a man. He went free at last, having served five or six years of a life sentence. Obviously there was some pretty serious perjury in his case, and if Bissert was concerned in it he did well to have a care for the righteous vengeance that hung over him.

Bissert was, moreover, much hated by the convicts for his rapacity. They charged him with being an insatiable hog and, while allowing pickpockets and other thieves to work under protection, was relentless in his demands for a "bigger corner" out of every "trick that was turned." Many queer stories were told—in his presence—of his crooked ways, in terms that made him writhe with helpless shame and fear. If ever a convict was wretched in Sing Sing and was despised and reviled by his fellows, Bissert was certainly that man. He did well to spare no effort to get out of a place where he must have suffered keenly. He couldn't pass through the yard without hearing the sharp hiss of some scornful thief shrilling in his ears, nor enter the mess-room without seeing a hundred fingers pointed at him in contempt and aversion. At night, in his cell, he could hear the taunts of the convicts in no restrained terms, one calling aloud some shameful story of his cruelty and crookedness, to be followed by another indignant victim reciting some black chapter of his career. In fact, policemen who get into state prison do not find their lives cast in pleasant places, but Bissert found his the hardest of any. It is not strange that he was willing to turn state's evidence rather than take a chance of coming back by the confirmation of his sentence in the Supreme Court.

From time to time Sing Sing has had some prisoners who, for a little while, at least, were prominent figures in the public eye, and nearly all the time there are two or three confined there whose notoriety is marked. Perhaps no one of them was more curiously asked after by visitors than John Y. McRane of Gravesend, and probably few men ever came to the prison who were so useful to the state. He was a competent builder and took charge of the construction of a new administration building, on which three hundred and fifty thousand dollars were expended. He drew the working plans, gave his attention to the work in detail and with a creditable industry and marked ability carried the building to completion. There were paid bosses and contractors on the job, but McRane ruled them all. His imprisonment, by reason of his industry, was therefore no particular hardship; at least, he did not feel it keenly because of the absorbing interest he took in his work. He was, in more ways than one, a model prisoner.

George W. Pell, the broker, who came back a second time, under circumstances that secured the sympathy of all who knew him and who is serving his term of three and a half years, was, more than any other one I knew, contented, light-hearted and apparently indifferent to his surroundings—and that, too, under conditions that could have excused another attitude. Perhaps it was only a mask, hiding all the care and sadness which he never revealed. He is a man of culture and refinement, a musician of high training, and he presided at the piano regularly in the chapel as well as at all entertainments. He is tremendously stout, but his full habit is no bar to his activity and goes far to preserve his appearance of real or assumed jollity and good humor.

William A. Moore, whose notoriety from a peculiar black-
mailing charge, in which a woman of wonderful seductiveness,
Faye Moore, figured, was a marked prisoner. His crime and trial
was dramatic, and his wife, who was also tried but finally released, attracted very general attention by her beauty and her
way of life, and spread something of the interest she awakened
over her husband. She secured a divorce from him later on and
was frequently heard of as a member of the "happy, happy chorus" in comic opera and in other unsavory ways. Moore fought
very strongly for his release, taking every advantage of the legal
technicalities of his trial, but in vain. When these were exhausted he appealed to Governor Odell for clemency, but was
curtly refused. Moore was, in addition to holding a consular
position at some of the South African ports, the friend and
business manager of "Kid" McCoy, the prize fighter. Like most
men associated with the ring, his bearing was supercilious and
arrogant—qualities that did him no sort of good in prison and
kept him more or less in hot water.

Moore's acquaintance with McCoy was a passport to the favor of the New York prisoners, who are to a man supporters of
the great art of boxing. It was curious to observe how accu-
rately they maintained an intimate knowledge of all that was
happening with the sporting fraternity, and how quickly they
obtained news of important fights. The bulletin boards, with
their messages framed in electric light on the front of the
newspaper buildings in the city, were not more prompt than
these sources of knowledge. For example, two great fights took
place in San Francisco, beginning so late that, with the difference of time against them, the early and regular editions of the
New York newspapers did not include the finishing rounds; but
at six o'clock, when the rising bell rang, news of the victories of
Jeffries and Young Corbett in the rounds was in every man's
mouth. How did they get it? It reminds one of the stories that
come out of the Dark Continent on the wings of rumor, borne
viewlessly, but supported as to facts by news arriving in regular
channels weeks later.

However, the prisoners got the news and possibly the mystery of their methods would prove to be none on examination. Among the convicted sports were many others besides Moore who had figured in the prize-ring with more or less success, in some cases prominently enough to have their names written in that book of fame called *Fistiana*. These divided honors with Moore, and, on the occasion of fights taking place, posed as oracles upon whose lightest utterances a crowd hung entranced. The animation on such days was very delightful to the inmates, who passed on each succeeding morsel of description with great satisfaction until every detail of the battle was a common possession.

Long before my time, Ferdinand Ward, ex-alderman, Henry Jaehne, the banker, Fisk, Ward's partner, Lloyd Haight, Alderman McQuade and "honest John" O'Neal, Sergeant Crowley and, before them, Edward Stokes, Frank Walworth, Simmonds, the policy man, who shot somebody, and many others, formed the apostolic succession of notorious inmates whose line is rarely if ever broken. The traditions of these shining lights of convict society take strange and interesting forms. It is told that Simmonds and Stokes shared apartments on the upper floor of the hospital, a suite of three rooms, which they furnished without regard to expense, notably with a vast icebox that was always kept filled with approved varieties. There they held open house for the keepers and selected visitors from the outside; and thither, under cover of the night, came also visitors who stole in secretly, holding their skirts so that their familiar *frou-frou* might not be heard, but who, just before morning broke, marched out of the prison singing and dancing with utter indifference as to who might see or hear, and were carried hilariously away in hacks.

At other times the prison doors opened for a little while to these choice spirits who went forth for an evening in civilian dress. It is not related that these enlargements were long continued, but it is part of the history of Sing Sing that on the evening of an opening of a publican's fine saloon half a dozen wealthy convicts were brought out under escort to add to the festivity by liberal expenditure and that nobody was disappointed. There were strange occurrences in those days in prison affairs. The bookkeeper of the prison was a convict named Ellis, a former resident of Yonkers and a man of substance and parts. He organized a scale of time, and a man could get a year off his sentence at from two hundred to five hundred dollars. He sold about two thousand years, sharing the profits with the administration or such part of it as it was necessary to take into confidence, before the plot was detected. Men escaped altogether of whom no trace has been found; other irregularities took place which would be impossible now, so it is not unreasonable to suppose that the favored prisoners named had things very much their own way.

Ferdinand Ward was, in a sense, my predecessor as prison printer. He was, however, the whole thing, compositor, pressman and devil, and the old press from which he used to kick off tags and letterheads is still in use in the prison printing establishment. Ward, Jaehne and Crowley are well remembered by the old convicts, of whom there are many—the dean of the faculty being William Kelly, who has served thirty-three years on a life sentence. Kelly is now eighty-three years old, but he expects to go out next week at the latest. Poor old chap! It has been next week for him for more than a quarter of a century. Next week has never come, but he is still cheery and hopeful, as strong as a bull, and as hungry as a hunter. His only infirmity is failing eyesight. Recently he obtained a pension for services as a coal-passer in the Civil War in the navy. He knew his name, but he couldn't recall that of his ship; but the records of the department contained the entry all right, relating how he was discharged by reason of illness, contracted while on duty. He draws eight dollars per month, but it brought next week almost within touch of Kelly's outstretched but trembling hand.

"Now the humbug will let me go. I'll be a charge on nobody now. I have enough to live on and I can work for twenty-five years yet."

Everybody is a humbug with Kelly, and has been so for twenty years. His crime was murder, of course, but it was so long ago that even justice must have forgotten and possibly forgiven it, although the remorseless clutch of the law still holds him fast.

They order these things better in some countries. A life sentence is terminable in England at the end of twenty years, unless there is some strong reason to the contrary; and no one ever serves longer than twenty years, even when under delayed sentence of death. In this country alone among civilized nations, a life sentence ends when its subject is for ever indifferent to its span.

An old lifer of interest is John Downing, who has served twenty-five years. He was a soldier of the Civil War, who was in no less than eighteen battles and was under fire a hundred times. He was at Antietam, Fredericksburg, Vicksburg, the Wilderness, Petersburg on to Sailor's Run, was wounded and honorably discharged and pensioned, and was sentenced for life for manslaughter before the law reducing the penalty to twenty years was passed. All the others on the same list were freed at the end of twenty years, but, for some reason, old John is held. He, too, has been prepared to go next week, certainly the week after that, for many years. He has money and friends, but they have not availed him anything!

Perhaps the most curious figure about the yard is James H. Riley, a runner for the farm and gardener's party, who goes in and out of the prison and up to the village at will. He has served more than nineteen years on a life sentence and is trusted unreservedly. It is reasonable that he should be, for Riley came to prison from the Putnam County jail, carrying his own commitment and making safe delivery of it and himself while the sheriff intrusted with that duty lay drunk in the sleigh. Riley is a negro, and long ago determined to go home by the governor's clemency next week. He has not found the governor in accord with him about the hoped for result, but perhaps some *next week* will bring joy to Riley's heart.

What dark chapters from real life could be dragged up from the records of the prison! What romantic histories have ingloriously closed there! What vain repentances, made too late, what shame, what sorrow, what vain regret! No dark shadow that can be cast on life would be lacking. But through all its clouds shines the radiant star of hope. There is probably no man whose evil case may have included all the miseries possible to the situation, even those who were prepared to go in a few hours to the electric chair, who did not turn his eyes toward its beneficent light and keep them fixed there to the last. There is no despair so dense that hope does not penetrate it; and I never met any one of the many who might reasonably be supposed to be prey to the one, that was not being cheered and lifted up by the other.

And yet how wasted much of this hope is, except in that it makes tolerable the moment! The most wretched convicts are those who hope continually to be released. Such was William Miller, the five hundred and twenty per cent quick-rich-syndicate man. Personally, Miller was a frail little chap with a whopper jaw, relieved by teeth of dazzling whiteness. He clung to the youthful memories of the Sunday-school in which he was a teacher at the time of his fall, and in such moments he was a frank, engaging youth full of sunny, laughing good-humor. Something would recall to his mind that he was a man of great affairs, since he had handled millions and signed himself banker. The transition from one state to the other was tremendously funny, but it gave evidence of the boy he was. I had a considerable degree of intimacy with Miller, and he offered in a small and colorless way a very fair replica of Doctor Jekyll and Mr. Hyde. He was sick most of the time, never very sick, but on some days worse than others, and then he was Doctor Jekyll. He would improve in health for a little while and then the malign presence of Mr. Hyde would assert itself.

Miller was the slave of hope. If it cheered him temporarily it cursed him altogether at the finish, for in obedience to its call he committed strange and reprehensible acts. He made a confession which was only half a confession. He malingered to the extent of staying in bed for nearly four years, in order to support his plea for a pardon upon the basis of broken health. Finally, all of these failing, he turned informer completely and went on the stand against Ammon, his coparcener in the syndicate. All of these things he did in the hope of getting out. It would have been far better that he should have taken up his prison life manfully and, coupling work with study, he would have found that the time sped on wings. He was still young and, although by no means ignorant, was only a little educated. He could have given to his six and a half years the value of a college course and finished them a scholar with real pretensions to knowledge, the possession of half a dozen modern languages, a thorough mathematical training, or almost anything within the reach of his really good but unformed capacities. He chose the other way and every waking hour was a day in its long weariness of hope deferred. He plotted and planned, studied new schemes and attempted to apply them when old ones failed, and wore himself out as he did the patience of his friends. He did everything he ought to do, making sacrifice after sacrifice, and didn't get out after all. It might be denied that his going on the stand to convict his old partner should be classed as the act of an informer. It could easily be a duty to do so under some conditions. A law-abiding man of principle couldn't do otherwise; but he couldn't justify the most patched-up old conscience, if his motive was like Miller's, to trade his own bonds and vacate his own place in prison and fill it with another victim.

I have seen many come to prison borne up by the hope of release so strongly that it became conviction, and as it was disappointed day after day they simply withered up and occasionally some of them died. There was Henry Ziemer, the divorce lawyer, who furnished co-respondents for referees' hearing both male and female, and who swore away the reputations of chaste women and honorable men by the hundred. He got ten years and he hoped to get out. He knew perfectly well that no plea he could make for a pardon had legs to stand on for a moment, so he retained a firm of really very eminent political lawyers, who have done a large and remunerative pardon brokerage, to get him out. They thought they could for one or two thousand dollars, cash down, and the rest as contingency on success. But Ziemer's case was utterly impossible. The governor wouldn't look at it for a moment, and even when it got near enough to the executive to elicit the order, "Take that away; don't let me hear that man's name!" Ziemer could not understand it, and kept on hoping as before. I left him in prison hoping still.

If I had had seventy-five chances in a hundred to get a pardon, I would not have accepted the wretchedness that goes with waiting for the issue; but that does not seem to be the view taken by most convicted men. The scheme of pardon is so feasible—it is only to induce one man to sign his name—it is so simple that they can't understand that the chances of being struck by lightning are vastly greater.

There is another suggestion arising in this connection and confirmed by my own experience in a hundred instances, in drafting petitions for pardon or commutation for fellow prisoners. They could, in many cases, have done it as well as I and some of them better, but if an Addison or a Milton had been available they would have gone to him. It is that a convicted man can not see the facts in his own case. He has no perspective upon it, and from excusing himself at first he becomes grounded in the beliefs he has declared so often. It is certain that no prisoner can tell the whole truth about his crime. He may start to relate it fully and truthfully, admitting in a word his guilt, but every word after that is the palliating excuse. The blame is shifted until, when the story is all told, the first admission stands denied. This is true in so many cases that the rule in my mind stands absolute. So this peculiar bias may be the result as much as the cause of hopes so often disappointed.

Part Three

LIFE BEHIND THE BARS

WHEN WE THINK OF LIFE in the nineteenth-century prison, we envision the lock-step marching in silence, the downward eyes, the harsh living conditions, and especially the punishments. To be sure, all these elements are present, but we tend to lose sight of the extreme tedium of life lived in a cell, as well as the minor things that make such a life livable. In many accounts, however, punishment and torture take precedence over other details of prison life by providing the reader with the sensational and gruesome details of convict life. This discourse is intentional because narratives of endless days and nights surely wouldn't sell in the marketplace. Boredom is rarely marketable. So although the ordinary was normative in the daily life of the prison, corporal punishment was certainly widespread in nineteenth-century prisons, and most convict-authors take note of the tortures in their particular penitentiaries. In our contemporary prison discourse we hear of a return to "no-frills" prisons. To us this means no amenities such as televisions, modern weight-lifting equipment, and other recreations. To the nineteenth-century convict, "frills" would have been a foreign concept with little meaning. Today we tend to lose sight of the brutality inflicted on prisoners in this "heroic" age of the American penitentiary. Take Seth Wilbur Payne's *Prison Diary,* for example. His daily account of life in prison includes many of the techniques used to make convict life intolerable. He writes of the cruelties of the "dungeon," general inhumane treatment, and prison's harshly negative effect on the human soul. D.B. Smith in *Two Years in the Slave-Pen of Iowa* provides more detail on specific punishments such as the "pulley" which distorts "every muscle a man has in him." Carl Arnold in *The Kansas Inferno* writes not only of corporal punishments but also those that deprive the convict of the few small privileges that make life sustainable behind bars. Julian Hawthorne's entry represents a special case in these narratives. Son of the famous American writer Nathaniel Hawthorne and a prolific writer himself, Julian edited *Confessions of a Convict* in 1893, a book in which he took a decidedly dim editorial view of convicts. But after he served one year in the Atlanta Penitentiary for mail fraud in 1913, he wrote *Subterranean Brotherhood*, which one critic characterized as "a self-righteous attack on imprisonment and society." The selection from *Confessions* gives his view before experiencing the pains of prison for himself.

The punishment component of doing time makes for good reading, but daily life goes on. John Reynolds, in *A Kansas Hell*, describes Sunday in prison and the modicum of relaxation the day provides. He then goes on to give one of the few contemporary descriptions of women in prison, with their jobs of sewing and washing, and a rare account of American Indian convicts. Most convicts devise survival strategies and the clever ones usually find a way to circumvent the rules. The nineteenth-century penitentiary had many more restrictions than our modern counterpart. Censorship of all types was common until Supreme Court decisions of the latter half of the twentieth century. Convicts couldn't write uncensored letters and prison libraries only provided approved reading materials. Determined prisoners usually found a way to smuggle messages. To cite but one example, counterfeiter and bank robber Langdon Moore writes of his ingenious scheme to communicate with his wife with messages on an envelope concealed by a stamp. Smuggling letters and books was benign compared to other prison contraband. Prisoners have found ways to use stimulants since the beginning of penitentiary life in America. Walter Wilson is only one convict among a host who gives a vivid description of narcotic habits either continued or begun in prison. Light-Fingered Jim, who was himself very fond of opium, writes in this selection of his strategy of reading that helped him get through the many dreary nights and years of confinement. Especially interesting is his personal take on literary characters from famous books. The author of *Prisoners of the Ohio Penitentiary* writes of convicts who both read and write fiction and verse. While the examples are perhaps not the best poetry, they do reveal some sincere sentiments of the incarcerated.

Most subcultures have their own colloquialisms. Criminals perhaps provide some of the most interesting slang that has entered our own spoken and written language. "Snitch" and "screw" are two of the best known expressions that survive to this day. Bunko Kelley and Prisoner Number 1500 provide some lively examples and translations for the general reader. From these narratives we get an intimate view of imprisonment in the nineteenth century, one that is found nowhere else.

Prison Diary

BY SETH WILBUR PAYNE

From *Behind the Bars* by Seth Wilbur Payne (New York: Vincent & Co., 1873).

Wednesday, April 24. I have once or twice alluded to the "dungeon" but never until today did I really understand what "punishment in the dungeon" meant. I supposed it was merely shutting a prisoner in a dark, damp place, where there was no bed or place to sit down, no light, no sound, no knowledge of whether it was night or day. Nothing to eat but a dry crust of bread, which I would either have to hold in my hand from meal to meal or run the risk of finding it in the dark. Thus shut up, cold, shivering, tired, sleepy, hungry, homesick and half dead in general, for from one to ten days I supposed to be the dungeon I heard so much about. Now, today I have learned it is not only this, but a great deal more. The prisoner is hung up by his wrists; the tips of his toes just touching the floor; then three thick, heavy doors are locked and bolted against him—and he is alone. The hours pass: his arms begin to swell, the heavy irons about his wrists stop the circulation of the blood and cut through the flesh to the bone. He moans piteously for help. He is dying from torture and cries for some one to save his life: but through the thick walls which surround him a cannon's boom could scarce be heard. He grows weaker and weaker. He feels the cords in his wrists and arms giving way; his head sways from side to side; his throat ceases to utter any but a gurgling sound; his eyes are set; a tremor runs through his whole frame; his head falls forward between his bleeding, swollen arms, and he is as unconscious of pain as he was before this awful punishment. And this in a civilized country! surrounded by praying parsons and a christian people! Shame on such a christianity! Shame be to such praying parsons, and shame to such a civilization!

Thursday, April 25. Nice day. The walls begin to warm through. The sun is shining on the world outside. We can smell

Spring though we can't see it. We know the grass is getting green on the lawn and in the pastures. The birds are choosing their mates and commencing to build their nests. The girls and the hired man are raking off the flower beds in the front yard. The farmers have finished sowing their spring wheat and are now plowing up the old meadow lot for corn. The sheep and young stock have been turned out to pick their living. The boats are making regular trips up and down the Hudson. The country merchants are busy measuring calico and cotton cloth and weighing out sugar and eight-penny nails. The school ma'ms are applying for the summer schools while the city girls are sighing for the season at Saratoga and the seashore. It does us good to imagine all this, though look where we can, naught but iron bars and ghost-like walls look back at us.

An old prisoner whispered to me this morning, "Ten weeks from to-day is the Fourth."

"Do you go out on the Fourth of July?" I inquired.

"Me, go out! Ha, no. I shall never go out till death calls me away. I am here for life."

"How long have you been here?"

"Going on fifteen years—let's see, this is '72 isn't it? I came in on the ninth day of November 1856. How many would that fetch it now—no, it's going on sixteen years, sure enough. I was thinking all the while 'twas fifteen."

"What makes you think of the Fourth of July more than any other day?"

"You'll see when it comes. We always have a good dinner on the Fourth. Lots of strawberries with sugar and milk, a piece of tender roast beef and some clean fried potatoes. We will have pies, puddings and sweet cakes, and some years we have ice cream and lemonade. You'll see. We never have to work on the Fourth. We go in the chapel the same as on Sundays, and some nice young ladies and gentlemen from the city come in and sing to us. Only ten weeks from to-day, sir. That's all. Just ten weeks. That will be—let me see: seven times ten are seventy— only seventy days. Soon come round now—'twill, sir. Yes, sir, soon come round now."

Yes, poor old man; bowed by years of hardship and toil, may God hasten the day—not the day of festivity of which you childishly speak, but that great day of deliverance. Oh death, more lovely than the spring time must be thy coming to one thus afflicted. Hasten thou to his relief. Strike from his trembling frame the shackles that for sixteen long years have chained him in to this place, and let the poor old captive go free.

Friday, April 26. It beats all, how a little practical knowledge will change a man's mind. What a difference there is between the ideal and the real. Two months ago, I was strongly of the opinion that it was wicked to hang a person up by the neck until he was dead. I thought it was unmerciful, barbarous and cruel. Now, since I have been shut up in a prison for eight weeks, partaking of a prisoner's fare, suffering his sorrows and sharing all his comforts; since I now know from experience what a prisoner's life is, I think it an act of great mercy to kill a man outright, all at once, either by choking, strangling, shooting, spearing, burning or cutting off his head, rather than shut him up in a cold, damp prison and torture him to death by inches. It would be an act of mercy for the State to take two-thirds of these prisoners and put an end to their misery by hanging them up by the neck or piercing their hearts with a rifle ball. When a horse falls down on Broadway, breaks a leg or is unable to get up, the first policeman that comes along, sends balls enough into his head to put the poor brute out of his misery. Now what is a horse better than we? Why should not the same christian feeling be shown towards us human animals? Hereafter, I shall advocate the death penalty in all cases where a man is found unfit to enjoy his liberty. As soon as a man be adjudged dangerous to run at large among men, kill him. If he is not fit to live in this world send him over to the next, for, see here, that which our law makers call crime is of the body and not of the mind. It comes from a torpid liver, a weak stomach or a wrongly educated brain. For all these the criminal is not to blame. Then why put him to torture for that which he cannot help. Because a person's body makes him dangerous why punish the soul? If the soul and the body be at variance, why not separate them? Thirty days in prison is long enough. If a man cannot be reformed in thirty days, show a little mercy towards the poor animal and kill him.

And this puts me in mind of saying a word about "prison reform." Of course I can only speak from eight weeks experience, but so far as my observation has extended, I have found the object of prison discipline or prison reform to be, to make convicts criminals instead of good citizens. I do not see how a young man could stay here two years without having all honest purposes in life burned out of him. Of course a strong will and established principles might escape, but the rule is that men are made vastly worse instead of better. No one ever mourned the loss of a son more than I, yet could I bring my little Wirtie back to me as he was a year ago by subjecting him to four months torture behind these bars, I would sooner his precious little body should continue to sleep on in that far distant grave where by strange hands he was laid. To strong, full grown men and women the tortures inflicted are not so appalling; but to see boys and girls hung up by their thumbs while the rats are gnawing at their feet, fainting in their cells for want of food, driven sick; and bleeding to the severest tasks; where is the parent who could witness this without cursing the God who brought man into being to suffer the tortures of a thousand hells; or where the father who would not sooner take the life of his own child, than see him writhe in such hellish agony.

Saturday, April 27. "Give me ticket to London. Ye got it for me. I'm all ready to start tomorrow." This is what I hear every time I pass one of the lower cells. It is uttered by a young man serving out a life sentence for murder. He is an Englishman; came to this country five years ago with his young wife whom he married the day before sailing. Leaving his bride at a third-rate boarding-house in New York, he sought employment as a gardener in one of the suburban towns. At the end of four weeks he returned just in time to learn that his wife had been faithless to him, in her devotion to a genteel young boarder of the same house. Stung to madness, he sought the destroyer of his happiness and hurled him into eternity by a single blow. After being in prison a couple months, word came to him that his wife had died of a broken heart. From that day he has been a raving maniac. He talks constantly about his "Sadie." He says she has gone to London, and he wants a ticket so he can go where she is. He thinks the prison door is closed against him because he has no ticket and his "Give me a ticket to London" falls on the ear of each passer by.

Again we ask why not take pity on this poor, pitiable human animal and give him a pass to his "Sadie" by way of a minnie ball. No one would consider it human to permit a dog to live under similar circumstances, and is a man's misery of less consideration than a dog's? As soon as this man was declared unfit or unsafe to live in this world, why was he not butchered on the spot? Who is it that delights in human torture? The savage who cuts away the life of his victim piece by piece, or burns him over a slow fire we cry out shame against, and yet, are we less savage? Do you say yes? Then come, stay six weeks a prisoner.

Look and see, and then decide whether we of the nineteenth century are civilized, half-civilized or a barbarous race.

Punishments

By D.B. Smith

From *Two Years in the Slave-Pen of Iowa* by D.B. Smith (Kansas City, Missouri: H.N. Farrey & Co., 1885).

There are various modes of punishing the refractory citizens of this institution, and also different degrees of punishment for different offenses committed or repetitions of the same. There used to be what they called the pulley punishment. This was a very severe ordeal to undergo. The culprit is handcuffed and the pulley hooked on between the cuffs. There are two blocks in the pulley, one of which is fastened in a horizontal beam some twenty feet above the floor, the other being loose to run up and down at will. All being ready, the officer whose duty it is to punish now pulls on the rope, and up and down goes the poor convict, like a jumping jack in a spectacular show. Some strong, nervy fellows can hold themselves in check from holloaing or crying, but it is seldom. Sometimes they will faint outright, when some water is thrown on to bring them to, and the punishment continued if not finished. If a fellow tries to hold in and fails he makes a heart-sickening noise, something like that of the neigh of a burning horse in his last moments. It is an awful ordeal for a man to go through, and must, without doubt, distort every muscle a man has in him. It was told me, by guard who had been in the institution a long time, that a deputy warden, some ten years ago, ran a woman up and down on this instrument of torture and beat her with his cane meanwhile. It seems too cruel to be true, and all I can say about it is, if it is true, that he ought to have been drowned. Let us hope that the story was repeated merely from hearsay, and not a fact. This mode of punishing was abolished by Mr. Crosley, or rather, suspended during his term of office, to be probably taken up again by the next man who comes in. Then there is what they call "the hole;" these were three cells made dark by fastening a piece of sheet-iron over the grating of the door, which made it perfectly dark in the cell; the boy or man was put in here for a certain length of time and fed on bread and water—not much bread, but plenty of water. He has nothing in this cell, no matter how long he stays, except his cell bucket and tin cup. In the center of the roof of one of these cells is a ring-bolt, and when one is to be punished somewhat harder than the mere confinement, handcuffs are put on, and he is chained up to that, his feet cleverly resting on the floor, and is kept there during the working hours of the day. For a lesser punishment they are chained up to the doors of their own cells during the day, and let down at night; in this event they have to live on bread and water, but can sleep in their own beds at night. There is also the ball and chain, but this is not much resorted to, for after a man carries this till his strength gives out it is merely impossible for him to continue. Latterly they have adopted a system of good behavior tickets. The convict is given four tickets—one entitles him to weekly tobacco, one to lamp in his cell, one to write letters, and one to see friends; these are taken away, one at a time, for certain offenses, and returned again at stated intervals. This ought to work very well, whether it does or not.

Sunday in the Prison

BY JOHN N. REYNOLDS

From *A Kansas Hell, or Life in the Kansas Penitentiary* by John N. Reynolds (Atchison, Kansas: The Bee Publishing Co., 1889).

A prisoner is always thankful for the Sabbath. He has been working hard all week and Sunday affords the opportunity of resting. On the Sabbath morning, the bell for rising rings at eight o'clock. At its ringing each person must rise and dress; he is not permitted to do so before it rings. If he gets tired of remaining in his bunk so late as eight o'clock, and should wish to get up and dress, it would do him no good; it would be a violation of rules and result in punishment. After the prisoner is up and dressed, he washes and marches out in ranks to breakfast. It is hash, hash, hash, for Sunday breakfast, the same as any other day, except once a month it is codfish hash instead of beef hash. After breakfast, instead of going from the dining room to work, the prisoners are marched back into their cells where they remain until time for chapel exercises.

There is a dining room for the prisoners and another for the officers. The room where the prisoners dine is a large hall capable of seating fully twelve hundred men. Each table is long enough to accommodate twenty men, and resembles an ordinary school desk. There are no table-cloths or napkins; nothing but a plain, clean board. The table furniture consists of a tin quart cup, a small pan of the same precious metal, which holds the hash, an iron knife, fork and spoon. No beautiful silverware adorns this table; on the contrary, all the dining service is very plain and cheap. The convicts are marched into the dining room in divisions and seated at the table. Here they remain in perfect silence with their heads bowed.

No talking or gazing about the dining room is permitted. After all the divisions are in and seated, the deputy warden taps a small bell, and the convicts begin the work of "concealing the hash." Before the men enter the dining room the coffee, bread and hash are placed on the table for each man. The prisoners are given all the food they can eat. It is not the quantity, but the quality, that is objectionable.

If more bread is wanted, instead of calling out "Please pass the bread," the convict holds up his hand and the waiter comes along and puts a piece of bread in it. He gets but a pint of coffee, and if he wishes a second supply he holds up his cup and it is refilled—but with water instead of coffee. If he wishes more hash he holds aloft his meat dish and an officer hands him a large pan of hash out of which he fills his dish. Not a word is spoken during the meal. Ample time is given the convicts to get all the food they desire; then the deputy warden, who occupies a raised seat at the end of the dining room taps a small bell and the men march out in divisions, back to their cells on Sunday mornings, and to their work on week days.

Breakfast over and the men in their cells, the choir, which leads the singing and furnishes the instrumental music for the occasion, is taken out, and, under the watchful care of an officer, is conducted to the chapel where they practice until time for the regular services. The choir was composed of convicts who could sing, regardless of the crimes for which they will be sent to prison. I recollect at one time we had two horsethieves, two rapists—one with a sentence of forty years, three murderers, two hogthieves and several others of equally villianous records, and last of all, the author! But this choir will compare favorably with some of the high-toned church choirs outside! To return, think of such a choir singing:

> *"Oh, how happy are they,*
> *Who their Savior obey,*
> *And have laid up their treasures above!"*

At eleven o'clock, the prison bell rings and the men are marched in the ranks to the chapel. When the first division or company reaches the room where the services are to be held, the string band commences to play, and as the divisions march in one after another they are greeted with music. The instruments used are a piano, organ, violin, cornet, and bass viol.

Very fine music is rendered by the prison band. All being seat-ed, the chaplain, the Rev. Dr. Crawford, a genuine Christian and God-fearing man, rises, and in his happy style reads some beautiful hymn which is familiar to the congregation. The choir leads and the entire congregation sings. Such singing! The convicts have only one opportunity a week to try their voices in a musical way, and when that opportunity comes around it is improved. Nearly one thousand voices unite in singing those beautiful gospel hymns! A prayer is offered; more singing; then the chaplain, or some visiting minister who may be present, preaches a short discourse. There is a large field for usefulness and for doing good in the penitentiary. The harvest is truly great. Chaplain Crawford comprehends the situation, and is putting forth strenuous efforts to save these men, who have drifted thus far down the currents of sin. His labors are abundantly blessed of God. Many men go out of that institu-tion a great deal better than when they first entered. Were it not for the cruel treatment the prisoners suffer in the coal mines of that institution many more of them would be re-formed. This treatment tends to harden the criminal. The chaplain has many evils to counteract, yet he contends nobly for the right, and some of these men are being redeemed from a sinful life. After the sermon, the choir and the string band furnish more soul-stirring music, which enlivens the spirits of the prisoners, and then the chapel exercises are over. The pris-oners are now returned to their cells. Occasionally the convicts are permitted to remain after the chapel exercises proper are over and have a social meeting. The chaplain remains with them. These men sing, pray and give in their religious experi-ence. It is novel to hear these Christian criminals telling how they love Jesus.

Immediately after the religious services are over the prison school begins. Nearly one hundred of the convicts attend this school. The common branches, reading, writing, spelling, arithmetic, etc., are taught. This school is graded, and under the management of the chaplain, who is an excellent instruc-tor, is a great blessing to the prisoners. Numbers have fitted themselves here so that when they went out they were able to pass examinations and obtain certificates as teachers.

On entering the institution many of the prisoners who are unable to read and write soon acquire these useful arts if they have any ambition for self-improvement. If there was room, and this school could be conducted in the evening, as well as on Sunday afternoons, much more good could be accomplished. I would suggest that it would be a good act on the part of the State to employ an officer who should devote all his time to teaching and imparting instruction in the common branches, and let a room be fitted up for evening school, so that all prisoners who might desire to improve themselves could attend this place of instruction after the work of the day was over. Nothing could be done that would he more advantageous to the convict. The teachers for the prison school are selected from among the prisoners, some of them being very fine scholars.

After school is over the Sunday dinner is served. The prisoners once more march into the dining room and take their places at the table. The Sunday dinner is the "crack" meal of the institution. At this meal the prisoners have as a luxury beans, a small piece of cheese and some beet pickles in addition to their regular diet. This meal is served at 2:30.

The prisoners are then returned to their cells, where they remain until the following morning. They spend their time in the cells which is not taken up by sleeping, in reading. The prison has a fine library of five thousand volumes. The State Legislature annually appropriates five hundred dollars to be expended in purchasing books. This collection consists of histories, scientific works and books of fiction. The greater part of the criminals prefer the works of fiction. Were it not for this privilege of reading, the Sunday afternoons and winter evenings would seem very long, and dreary. Several officers are on duty during the time the men are locked in their cells on Sunday, and the cell houses are very quiet and orderly. There is no talking, as officers are constantly walking backwards and forwards in front of the cells.

This is the manner and style of spending the Sabbath in

prison. The convicts who do the cooking for the officers and convicts are compelled to work on Sundays as any other day of the week. It would be nothing more than right to give these men credit for this extra work and in this manner reduce their sentences. The law does not contemplate that criminals in the penitentiary should work seven days in the week and fifteen hours each day. There are more than fifty men who are forced to put in this extra time in hard labor.

The Prisoners

By John N. Reynolds

From *The Twin Hells: A Thrilling Narrative of Life in the Kansas and Missouri Penitentiaries* by John N. Reynolds (Chicago: The Bee Publishing Co., 1901).

Thinking as it may be interesting to some of my readers, I will now give, in brief form as possible, a history of some of the most noted inmates of the penitentiary

Female Convicts

He must be of a very unsympathizing nature who does not feel for his brother, who, though deserving, is imprisoned and excluded from the society of friends. While we are sad when we behold our fellowmen in chains and bondage, how much sadder do we become when passing through the prisons, we behold those of the same sex with our sisters, wives and mothers. In this land, blessed with the most exalted of civilization, woman receives our highest regard, affection and admiration. While she occupies her true sphere of sister, wife or mother, she is the true man's ideal of love, purity and devotion. When, overcome by temptation, she falls from her exalted sphere, not only do men feel the keenest sorrow and regret, but, if it is possible, the angels of God weep.

In the Kansas penitentiary, just outside the high stone wall, but surrounded by a tight board fence some fifteen feet high, stands a stone structure—the female prison. In this lonely place, the stone building, shut out from society, there are thirteen female prisoners. During the week these women spend their time in sewing, patching and washing. But very few visitors are allowed to enter this department, so that the occupants are permitted to see very few people. Their keepers are a couple of Christian ladies, who endeavor to surround them with all the sunshine possible. For these inmates the week consists of one continual round of labor. It is wash, patch and sew from one year's end to the other. The Sabbath is spent in reading and religious exercises. In the afternoon the chaplain visits them and preaches a discourse. Several of these women are here for murder. When a woman falls she generally descends to the lowest plane.

A few days before I was discharged, there came to the prison a little old grandmother, seventy years of age. She had lived with her husband fifty-two years, was the mother of ten children, and had fifteen grand-children. She and her aged husband owned a very beautiful farm and were in good circumstances, probably worth $50,000. Her husband died very suddenly. She was accused of administering poison. After the funeral, she went over into Missouri to make her home with one of her married daughters. She had not been there but a short time when her eldest son secured a requisition, and had his aged mother brought back to Kansas and placed on trial for murder. She was convicted. The sentence imposed was one year in the penitentiary, and at the end of which time she was to be hung by the neck until dead, which in Kansas is equivalent to a life sentence. The old woman will do well if she lives out one year in prison. She claims that her eldest son desires her property, and that was the motive which induced him to drag her before the tribunal of justice to swear her life away. During her long life of three score and ten years, this was the only charge against her character for anything whatever. She always bore a good name and was highly esteemed in the neighborhood in which she lived.

Another important female prisoner is Mary J. Scales. She is sixty-five years of age, and is called Aunt Mary in the prison. She is also a murderess. She took the life of her husband, and was sentenced to be hung April 16, 1871. Her sentence was commuted to a life imprisonment. For eighteen years this old woman has been an inmate of the Kansas penitentiary. While she is very popular inside the prison, as all the officers and their families are very fond of Aunt Mary, it seems that she has but few, if any, friends on the outside. Several old men have been pardoned since this old woman was put into prison, and if any more murderers are to be set at liberty, it is my opinion that it will soon be Aunt Mary's turn to go out into the world to be free once more.

Mrs. Henrietta Cook

This woman was twenty-five years of age when she came to the Kansas penitentiary to serve out a life sentence. She was charged with having poisoned her husband. For fifteen years she remained in close confinement, at the end of which time she received a pardon, it being discovered that she was innocent. When Mrs. Cook entered the prison she was young and beautiful, but when she took her departure she had the appearance of an old, broken-down woman. Fifteen years of imprisonment are sufficient to bring wrinkles to the face, and change the color of the hair to gray. This prisoner made the mistake of her life in getting married. She, a young woman, married an old man of seventy. She was poor, he was rich. After they had been married a short time she awoke one morning to find her aged husband a corpse at her side. During the night he had breathed his last. The tongue of gossip soon had it reported that the young and beautiful wife had poisoned her husband to obtain his wealth, that she might spend the rest of her days with a younger and handsomer man. After burial the body was exhumed and examined. The stomach showed the presence of arsenic in sufficient quantity to produce death. The home of the deceased was searched and a package of the deadly poison found. She was tried, and sufficient circumstantial evidence produced to secure her conviction, and she was sent to prison for life. A short time before this sad event happened, a young drug clerk took his departure from the town where the Cook family resided, where he had been employed in a drug store, and took up his abode in California. After fifteen years of absence he returned. Learning of the Cook murder, he went before the board of pardons and made affidavit that the old gentleman was in the habit of using arsenic, and that while a clerk in the drug store he had sold him the identical package found in the house.

Other evidence was adduced supporting this testimony, and the board of pardons decided that the husband had died from an overdose of arsenic taken by himself and of his own accord. The wife was immediately pardoned. How is she ever to obtain satisfaction for her fifteen years of intense suffering? The great State of Kansas should pension this poor woman, who now is scarcely able to work; and juries in the future should not be so fast in sending people to the penitentiary on flimsy, circumstantial evidence.

The other female prisoners are nearly all in for short terms, and the crime laid to their charge is that of stealing.

Indians in the Penitentiary

John Washington and Simmons Wolf are two young Indians tried and convicted in the U.S. District Court on the charge of rape. They were sentenced to be hung. After conviction these Indians were taken to the penitentiary to await the day set for their execution. In the meantime an application was made to the President to change the sentence of death to that of life imprisonment. The change was made. These two Indians were placed in the coal mines on their arrival, where they are at the present time getting out their daily task of coal. They both attend the school of the prison, and are learning very rapidly. Prior to this, Washington served out a one-year sentence in the Detroit house of correction for stealing. He is a bad Indian.

At present there are fourteen Indians incarcerated in the Kansas penitentiary. The Indian pines for his liberty more than the white man or negro. The burdens of imprisonment are therefore greater for him to bear.

One young Indian was sent to the penitentiary whose history is indeed touching. Ten Indians had been arrested in the Territory by U.S. marshals for horse-stealing. They were tried and convicted in the U.S. District Court. Their sentence was one year in the State's prison. On their arrival at the penitentiary they were sent to the mines to dig coal. This was a different business from being supported by the government and stealing horses as a diversion. The Indians soon wanted to go home. One of them was unable to get out his task of coal. The officer in charge thought he was trying to shirk his work and reported him to the deputy warden. The young Indian was placed in the dungeon. He remained there several days and nights. He begged piteously to get out of that hole of torture. Finally the officers released him and sent him back to the mines. While in the dungeon he contracted a severe cold. He had not been in the mines more than a couple of days, after being punished, when he gave suddenly out and was sent to the hospital, where in a few days he died. That young Indian was murdered, either in that dungeon or in the mines. A few weeks before, he came to the penitentiary from roaming over the prairies, a picture of health. It did not take long for the Kansas penitentiary to "box him up" for all time to come. He now sleeps "in the valley," as the prison graveyard is called.

Another one of the same group did not fare quite so badly as his associate. The one I am now describing was sent with the rest of his companions to the bottom of the mines. He remained there during the first day. A short time after he went down on the following morniing he became sick. He began to cry. The officer in charge sent him to the surface. He was conducted to the cell-house officer, Mr. Elliott. I was on duty that day in the cell house, and Mr. Elliott, on the arrival of the Indian, ordered me to show him to the hospital After we had started on our journey from the cell house to the hospital building to see the doctor, and had got out of hearing of the officer, I said, "Injun, what's the matter with you?" This question being asked, he began to "boo hoo" worse than ever, and, rubbing his breast and sides with his hands, said, between his sobs, "Me got pecce ecce." I was not Indian enough to know what "pecce ecce" meant. In a few moments we reached the hospital building, and I conducted my charge into the nicely furnished room of the prison physician, and into the immediate presence of that medical gentleman. Removing my cap, and making a low bow, as required, I said, "Dr. Nealley, permit me to introduce a representative of the Oklahoma district, who needs medical attention."

While I was relieving myself of this little declamation the young Indian was standing at my side sobbing as if he had recently buried his mother.

"Reynolds, what is the matter with him?" asked the doctor.

I then turned to my charge and said, "Injun, tell the doctor what ails you."

Mister Indian then began rubbing his sides and front, with tears rolling down his face, and sobbing like a whipped schoolboy, he exclaimed, "Me got pecce ecce."

"There, doctor," said I, "you have it. This Indian has got that dreadful disease known as 'pecce ecce.'"

The physician, somewhat astonished, informed me that he never had heard of such a disease before. I was in a similar boat and had never heard of such words prior. The sick Indian was unable to talk the language of the white man. The doctor then sent down into the mines for another of the Indians who could speak English and had acted as an interpreter. On entering the office, the doctor said to him, "Elihu," for that was his name, "this Indian says he has an attack of pecce ecce; Now what does he mean by that?"

During all this time the sick Indian kept rubbing his body and sobbing. It was of great astonishment and amusement when the interpreter informed us that "pecce ecce" meant nothing more nor less than "belly-ache." The doctor administered the proper remedy for this troublesome disease, and the Indian was sent back to the mines. He had not dug coal more than an hour when he had another attack and began his crying, and was sent to the top. He kept this up until he wore out the patience of the officers, and they finally decided to take him out of the mines altogether and give him work at the surface. Even here, every few minutes the Indian would have an attack of "pecce ecce," and would start for the hospital. At last, the chaplain, taking pity on the poor outcast, wrote to President Cleveland, and putting the case in a very strong light, was successful in securing a pardon for the Indian. That "cheeky" red youth was no fool. He belly-ached himself out of that penitentiary. I trust I may never have to spend any more of my time in prison. If I do, I think about the first day I will get a dose of "pecce ecce," and keep it up, and see if I can't get a pardon.

Under a Stamp

By Langdon W. Moore

From *Langdon W. Moore: His Own Story of His Eventful Life* by Langdon W. Moore (Boston: Langdon W. Moore, 1893).

Things ran along nicely for three years, and at the expiration of that time I had learned to make any kind of wagon or sleigh produced by the shop. Then my trouble commenced. The Warden and the inspectors discovered the State was losing money boarding the officers for three dollars a week; and as they would pay no more, they were given notice to find board and lodging elsewhere. When this was done, I was compelled to fall back upon such stuff as could be purchased at the store. The Warden's son was allowed ten per cent upon all such purchases.

It happened that Hank Hall of New York had deposited one thousand dollars in cash, to be given to any man who would get "Dutch Dan" pardoned out. As this could not be done without some reasonable excuse to take to the Governor and Council, he was allowed to write a letter to the president of every bank he had looked over in Maine, giving each of them a full description of the interiors, as well as the outsides, of their institutions. He also attempted to show the weakness of the work, and how the officials could make their banks absolutely safe against the attacks of burglars. This was soon noised about among the bankers all over the State, and made "Dutch Dan" very popular. As soon as the "coppers " who were to get the one thousand dollars were able to get in their work, and after Dan had been furnished with a model prison record, he was pardoned, without a single protest being made public.

Seeing what was done in this case, I thought it might be done in mine; and as no opportunity had ever been given me to speak a word to my wife privately during any one of her visits, I decided to communicate with her privately. This I did by writing twenty words on the outside of the envelope in a space that could be covered by a postage stamp. I would then put the stamp on and see that everything appeared regular. When these letters reached her, all she had to do was to put the envelope in water, and in a moment the stamp would be taken off and the envelope laid aside until the next letter came. In this way, in a few months, she received my instructions to raise twenty-five hundred dollars. When she had done this, she was to visit me, without mentioning the fact to me what she was going to do or telling me she had the money. With this she was to go to the Warden's wife, show her the money, and ask her where was the best place to put it to do me the most good in effecting my release.

She saw five men who agreed to put up five hundred dollars each; but just at this time Ned Lyons made his escape from Sing Sing Prison. He heard one of the men talking the matter over with some outside party, and knew that if this thing got noised about, the chances were against my being pardoned. I had not spoken to him for years, and we were not friends; but he went to my wife and put twenty-five hundred dollars in her hands. He then accompanied her to Bath, Me., where he remained while she came to the prison to see me.

In her anxiety to let me know she had raised the money, she foolishly wrote on the border of the New York Ledger, which she was allowed to send me weekly, these words: "All right. I will be there the second week in March." This was seen by the Warden before he allowed the paper to be sent to me in the prison. That night, upon her arrival at the prison, I was called up and shown into the room where I always went to see her. Here I saw her seated with the Warden, as on all previous visits. Not a word was spoken about the attempt being made for a pardon or the money, but this she managed to let me see in a small roll inside the cuff under her sleeve, without attracting the attention of the Warden. I was given the usual hour, during which I noticed the Warden seemed nervous, restless, and more watchful than ever before.

The following night I was again called up into this room. Seeing my wife was not there when I entered, I asked the Warden where she was, and was told she had gone back to New York. I asked why she had done this. He answered by asking me if he had not always been liberal with me in my correspondence. I replied that he had never given me any cause to complain. He then told me he had sent for my wife to come to his office at ten o'clock that morning, and asked her to tell him all about our private correspondence, who the man was that had taken the letters out of the prison for me, mailed them to her, and brought her answers to me in the prison. She had assured him she never received any letters from me except what came through the regular way. He then told her that unless she made a full confession and told him all about it, she could never see or hear from me again while I remained in prison under his charge. He had even locked the office door, thinking to intimidate her. Then he was told by her she had always taken him to be a gentleman, but now she saw her mistake; she asked him what kind of a reception I might expect, when I came home, from a wife who would come there and betray her husband, even admitting letters had passed between us without his knowledge or consent, which had not been the case.

"Now," he said to me, "I shall tell you the same as I told your wife: that unless you make a full confession to me and tell me who it was that carried out your letters and mailed them and brought her answers back to you, and make an apology to me for what you have done, you can never write to or receive a letter from your wife or any other person while you remain under my charge. Neither can you receive visitors or be allowed money or anything else that may be sent to you by your wife or any other person."

I replied: "My wife is not under your control, since you unlocked the prison door and allowed her to escape from your office. She has committed no breach of discipline. If one had been committed, I alone would be responsible to you for the acts of my wife while under my control, and you will never receive either a confession or an apology from me. This you can write down in the prison book in large letters, that every one who can see may read my answer to you."

I had served out but half of my sentence at this time, but I returned to my cell, determined to worry him a little while he was torturing me. I had a little money on me at this time, and made the attempt to make some small purchase by order at the store, but was told by the deputy I must see the Warden.

I waited patiently several months, and continued to buy paper, envelopes, and stamps. I wrote a letter to my wife every Sunday, knowing it would not be mailed.

No letters from her were ever allowed to reach me, and I was forced to live strictly on prison fare. This soon brought on dyspepsia, and I was compelled to see the doctor and get permission from him to be allowed hardtack. This I ate, without taking any other food, for ten months, and worked every day at my bench. At the expiration of that time I was well, and could eat any kind of food.

Persons and Things "In"

By Julian Hawthorne

From *The Confessions of a Convict; Illustrations from Life,* edited by Julian Hawthorne (Philadelphia: Rufus C. Hartranft, 1893).

Every morning, after mess, the hospital-bell sounds through the corridors. Captains unlock the catacombs of inmates who desire to see the "sawbones." All fall in line under the guard of the screw.

The hospital call is abused by many; consequently not a few inmates who are really ill are debarred from getting medical attention. Decent people prefer to suffer rather than go through the labor of getting treatment, and they often die in their vaulted, seven-by-four space. Sensitive zebus—and even animals have sensations—cannot endure the confinement in dungeon vile required previous to medical examination. The major cannot help this injustice. Don Juan M.C. rarely discriminates.

When No. 19,759 was leader of the swell company under Gentleman Allen's captaincy, a tall, angular Negro kid was admitted who was ill when he came. He had some disease of the stomach. Captain Allen, who is humane, allowed him up, the first day, to see the "croaker."

It is risky to tackle the croaker as soon as one arrives, no matter how ill one may be. This is the case in all penal catacombs. This Negro could not eat the food provided at mess, and consequently he ate nothing. Don Juan M.C. notified the captain "not to allow the Negro kid up to bother them, as nothing could be done for his case." These were the exact words.

Cap. was powerless to act. On the third day the kid could not get out of his cot, and could hardly fetch his breath, poor boy! One week from his arrival, he died alone, in intense agony, in the seven-by-four stone vault in which he could not breathe. It was a hard fate for a hale zebu like him—struggling against fate, dying there between damp stones. His death-throes and final gasp could be heard by his next-door neighbor. He was too weak to cry aloud for succor, but they shook their bars and shouted for aid: "Man off! Take him out!" The yell awoke Condom; the dread voice gains in volume. The sneaks sneaked up and unbarred the door, after a long delay to procure the key from front. Before they got him out that caged zebu was off—eternally off—gone to meet his Maker. No. 19,759 can plainly see the guards as they lug the dead weight past his room. The catacomb gas-jet illumines the scene, casting a ray on the ghastly, hideously contorted, upturned face. The procession winds down the middle stairway, facing cell 3z, where 19,759 stands at the bars. The two robust guards shudder in the presence of death, and try to hide their burden as they stagger by. Condom is wide awake; all view the scene with softened eyes.

I can never forget the look of agony stamped on that poor Negro boy's face. I recall it in the night: it is burnt into my memory. It is a stern, naked reality in this nineteenth century. I wonder if Don Juan M.C. ever stops to realize that he must render an account at the Great Day, when mundane accounts must be balanced justly. I wonder if that Negro boy's face of dead anguish ever visits Don Juan M.C. in his sleep? "Screwdom" could unfold many such another tale that would harrow the heart of man to hear; but their lips are closed. Were they to speak, off would go their official heads, and their families would be left without bread and butter.

No tales are ever told in the upper sphere. Discharged Condom is handicapped. Crooks, as a rule, dare not talk: their daily life is too crooked; their chief aim is to avoid publicity. Don Juan M.C. is fully aware of this important fact; hence there is no redress for murder "in." Condom must silently bear and suffer. If all the striped beings who have breathed their last in these catacombs could be ranged in single file, their number would appall humanity. This concerns all men. Every blood-curdling, inhuman act hurts mankind as a whole. What affects one affects all in time, the rich as well as the poor. When the sentence has been served, Copper John's disentombs a live human microbe, which comes in contact with those in the upper strata of life and affects their condition.

If the "in" croakers could be freed from the control of Don Juan M.C., whom all screws detest for his coarseness and inhumanity, the atmosphere of the catacomb would become healthier, and the outer world would be the gainer in the end. Scientific men should give heed to this subject. What concerns one microbe concerns all.

Lifer Burdick—Here is a creature that has been entombed for twenty years. You cannot any longer call it a man: it is an "it." It was once a jeweller and watchmaker. It worked honestly and hard to provide for its wife. The wife proved false—an old story; the husband found her out and killed her.

It is now a muffled-up mummy. It is always clad in a woollen scarf wrapped about the head and face. It never looks to right or left. It glides along, silently and alone, by the yellow-clay dead wall; the color of its skin is just like that of the wall. It is a gliding, automatic machine with a number. It is a skeleton in its shroud, actually decaying before your eyes. Not a ray of hope ever illuminates its features. It is a ghastly thing, legally dead and buried long ago.

It works in its cell for the officers, and they say it is a first-rate workman. Catacomb work by a ghost!

Lifer Jim King—Jim King is a graft. His place is called "King's Palace." He is tall, and thin as a rail. He is naked, except for a pair of trousers. He has a long, fiery-red beard. He never wears a cap. During the thirteen years he has lived at Copper John's the sun has given his skin the hue of copper.

He was a lawyer by profession. He shot his wife's paramour.

When he first came here they thought he was a skeleton articulated by some scientist. "Is he alive?" the agent asked. "Can you eat?" inquired the croaker. "Can you walk?" said the captain. "He stumps Barnum hollow," remarked a guard. The croaker decided that if he were alive, he could not long remain so. But croakers are not, it seems, always infallible in their diagnoses.

In a bag swung across his shoulder King carries a large black tom-cat, ferocious to every one, even to him. It is his pet, and as fiery in nature as is his own long red beard. King is the scholar of Copper John's. He is a king in the privileges he enjoys. His shrill voice can be heard all over Copper John's as he greets the captains and guards. He has sole sovereignty over the palace and the area adjoining it. He has a stove, and a table with books on it, and writing materials. Beneath is a cellar for provender. There is a hen-coop in the area; when the cock crows, the hayseeds all over the place laugh and nudge one another. He has a vegetable-garden, where he cultivates many choice vegetables. He is clean crazy, though he would not harm a sparrow. Were he sane, he would have been pardoned long ago. But he seems content, and is Copper John's most joyous inmate.

After his day's labor is over he can be seen sitting at his palace window, north, enchained to his books. A grape-vine drapes the palace. He has educated his two sons at college with money made "in" at contract work and by selling his garden-produce. He is still bony, but he is a healthier skeleton than he was.

Lifer Bill Comstock— Comstock is the veteran of the lifers. For thirty years he has been legally entombed alive. His face is the color of a corpse. He is a slim, nervous, silent semblance of a human being, who daily mopes about the grass-plot in front of the tailor-shop. He rarely lifts his eyes from the ground: when he does, you see a keen, dark, deep-sunken, fearless eye, with a hopeless gleam in it, savage in its intensity. He enjoys special privileges; he never has been ill, nor has he ever, during his siesta "in," given the officials any trouble.

The story of his prehistoric crime causes the creeps to penetrate the spinal column even of Condom. Condom shuns him. Its verdict on him is, "hanging would be too good for him." Condom's verdicts are square.

Comstock, incited to frenzy, perhaps by opium or rum, assaulted his aged parents and butchered them. He then calmly chopped up their bodies into steaks and ate them; and his appetite not yet appeased, he cut out their hearts, cooked them, and—horror of horrors—ate them! Yes, ate the hearts which used to feel for him—the heart that beat over him before he was born! That very atrocity saved his life. No doubt he knew it would. Maudlin humanitarians would not believe that such a wild beast could be sane. Since he was jailed, petition after petition has been signed and presented for his release. But his sister objects. She wants to live. He would swallow her at one gulp if he got the chance.

Don Juan M.C. has his eye on Comstock's stiff. The croakers offer a premium for it. He feels that no one "in" cares, and he looks like a walking automatic ghoul.

The Three Cruelties—These are all lifers. Two are Italians; the other is a pure-blooded Greek. All are chunky types of animation, swarthy, thick-set, hardy, low-browed, brutish. Lifer Antonio, the Greek, is the best of the trio. His mouth is stupidly open; he smiles childishly at every one who speaks to him.

Rega, one of the Italians, wears a murderous scowl on his repulsive mug. He looks murder: it is stamped on every act and thought; he cares for nothing but torture and bestiality. He belongs to a secret society, the Mafia. He is the type of the dyed-in-the-wool villain we read of history—a creature to be hired for a song to do foul murder. His crime was one of the most brutal and cold-blooded on record. He was twice sentenced to be hanged, but the Mafia saved his neck. Only the other day clerk Childs called him up to the desk and notified him that an application for his pardon had been made to Governor Hill.

Fusti, the third "cruelty," is a massy hulk of soulless matter; he is like an ox: he wants to eat, sleep, and loaf. All these "lock-step" in the swell company. They have been legally buried only since 1885.

Lifer John Welch—John is a mason by trade, an Irishman by birth, and a good Roman Catholic by faith. He is a massive, ox-necked, big-chested, open-hearted con. He is polite and diplomatic (who ever met a true-blooded Irishman that was not?);

he has been "in" six years, and feels his fate. He is rugged and the picture of robust health. He has a brood of little ones outside, whom he bears in mind on Christmas, and sends them all gifts he has made for them, marked "from papa." According to his own story, while crazed with rum he kicked or struck his wife, and she died. He hopes for a pardon after ten years. His conscience pricks him: one can tell that from his features. He once said to me, "It's my stomach that troubles me, boy."

It's your conscience, John, that is stabbing your inner, higher self.

Bathroom and Art-gallery—Copper John's bathing establishment is under the charge of lifer Pat Crowley, who has been "in" twelve years. It adjoins the ice-house, and both face the dead wall, in the second roadway south.

Crowley is always attended by his twin black spaniels, who are the pets of all Condom. He is a stout, stoop-shouldered, reticent, illiterate "trusty" (informer), and the major swears by him.

The bath-house has twenty-two iron bath-tubs, and soft soap is furnished *ad libitum*. A large vat overhead supplies hot water, which comes from the kitchen eastward. Companies bathe weekly in hot weather, and in winter every two weeks. Three captains superintend the bathing of Condom. One guards the bath-house; another unlocks the rooms; the third marshals Condom back and forth in lock-step file. Twenty-two are bathed at a time.

After bathing in hot water, in cold weather companies get chilled through standing in a line in the open air waiting for all to fall in. Many cons contract six-feet-of-earth colds; most of them have to come half naked, as little or no time to bathe is allowed, especially when Cerberus Bray is on duty.

Copper John's art-gallery occupies the walls of the bathhouse. Great rafters support the massive roof, under which hang life-size pictures, in order, with walnut frames. One would naturally look for classical subjects in connection with public baths; but Copper John's taste is modern. There are portraits of noted ballet-dancers from the Black Crook; actors of prominence—

Kean, Forrest, Booth, Jefferson, Barrett, Lester Wallack. There is a picture of Barnum's Hippodrome, and representations of famous horses, such as Flora Temple, Dexter, Maud S. There are statesmen also, many of them well known "in" for shady acts. And there they have hung for many a long "stretch."

Mess-room Drill—The captain, at his raised desk, rings a bell ten minutes before the order to fall in, to allow Condom time to wash up for mess. During these ten minutes cons are permitted to "chin their pals" in a whisper. At the order "fall in!" every con takes his accustomed place in company file, and all talk ceases. In dead silence the B-line of one hundred beings with souls is formed, all faces being toward the left while forming in the shop; at all other times faces are kept to the right. Cap. counts the figures in the line, then gives the order, "Steady—march!" The leader gives the slow-time step, and off they go, locked together compactly. Going down stairs this compactness is necessarily relaxed, but they close up again on reaching the level, and march along with a long, swaying thud, like the single tread of a giant. Shaky old cons and "silk-lined" ones are allowed to straggle at rear of company. The major stands at the steps leading up from the yard to his office, and reviews all tile companies as they pass by to mess.

Along the narrow passages between the benches of the mess-room the file goes at a slow step. A tin platter and cup and an iron-handled knife and fork are placed for each con. Under each bench are seventeen stools; the captains, who are the first to enter the mess-room, tell off the same number of cons, till all the stools are occupied. They then report "correct" to the major at his desk. The gallery waiters report the number on their galleries. The hospital count is added. If all are accounted for, the major hangs out a banner meaning "right!" Should the count not tally, no one can leave mess until it is made square.

The order to rise and march out is given by the major with a tap of his cane. The signal is repeated by the captains nearest the entrance on both side-aisles. Dead silence prevails: no order is given verbally. All is done by one-two taps of the cane. The only sound audible among twelve hundred human beings is the rattling of knives and forks, and the rippling wavelets of mastication when the meat is tough. To an on-looker it would seem like an asylum of mutes. Still, chin goes on, after the con-ish fashion, but inaudible to the uninitiated.

The bill of fare at morning mess is hash a la White, boot-leg (burnt stale bread in hot water), and bread. The hash is made of bread and grease, with rarely a tincture of meaty substance. At noon mess there is soup a la White, salt horse, and two spuds (potatoes) per man. On Fridays, cod-fish. Every other day there are pork and beans at noon mess, but never in the morning.

White, the steward, has amassed a competence by robbing the stomachs of his caged fellow-beings of the proper food needed to maintain life, and allowed each inmate by the State of New York. The food is not fit to feed swine on.

Should a con want to leave his bench for a drink of water, he raises his hand to the monitor, as he used to do at school. The monitor nods, and leave is granted. It is mutually under-stood that no undue length of absence is allowed. Mess over, Condom marches back to its workshops or to its cells, as the case may be, and silence reigns once more.

Condom's Letters — The days for receiving letters are Wednesdays and Saturdays, after one o'clock P.M. Oliver Cromwell, the clerk, brings each company's mail, tied up in a separate package, to the captain, who distributes it. If people who know cons "in" could see their radiant faces when they re-ceive a "stiff" (as a letter is called in Copper John's) and the glances of longing and envy of those who get none, they would be stimulated to perform an act of Christian charity by writ-ing to them.

Oliver Cromwell is a prim, puritanical bloke, whom Condom dislikes cordially because he is a "trusty." He used to run a hay-seed bank in his puritanical way; and he ran it so well that his bucolic depositors are still in search of what they put into it. The former clerk was bounced for mailing a stiff for a prisoner on the sly. Stiffs are often transmitted from one cell to another, "via rapid transit," to the profound mystification of the officials.

Each con, as a rule, has a cupboard that locks, in which he stores eatables and other things. Search-parties dare not break into these unless ordered to do so by the major or the warden. If they did, they would arouse the dead voice. The major, as a wise diplomat, knows how to rule his inmates humanely.

Prisoners from the bucolic districts who have wives generally hear unpleasant news about then after the first year or so. They seldom are faithful to the imprisoned ones more than a year and a half. The latter can tell from the tone of the letters that their wives want their freedom. There is only one living thing on earth who stands as firm as a rock to the con "in," and that is his mother. But the wives of regular crooks are, as a rule, faithful.

Cons are allowed to write once in two weeks, but after a "siesta" of a few years they seldom write at all.

The captains keep the letter-paper and the tab-cards. The chaplain reads the letters, stamps them, and mails them. The con writes the address of the letter at the right-hand top corner of the note paper.

Condom receives its letters minus the envelopes. If the letters contain objectionable matter, the inmates never receive them. In case there is urgent need to send a letter, special permission can be obtained by going up on certain days to the chaplain's office.

Hayseeds — Crooks in general evince a bitter aversion to prisoners from the bucolic districts. The latter betray "in" the same petty, underhand, and unmanly traits that characterize them outside. Farmers, as a rule, are the first to hinder a convict's escape. That is all right. Still, if the escaping convict offers them money they will accept it; but then, very likely, they will inform on the poor, hounded devil afterward, and so secure the State reward of fifty dollars into the bargain.

On the other hand, there is a free-masonry among crooks. They act square to their pals, both outside and "in." No amount of money will induce a thoroughbred crook to do a mean act to his craft. Caged humanity is sacred to crookdom. But this is not the case with the bucolic members of Condom. They are always ready to spy on their fellows, and in this way they obtain grafts and sinecures. They would betray their flesh and blood, and they constantly do so. Yet one would suppose that they ought to be imbued with higher aspirations than those who from birth have followed a crooked path, who never breathed a pure air, but are immured all their lives in an atmosphere of pollution. Bucolic inmates "squeal" whenever they can better themselves thereby; it matters not whom they injure. The officials, knowing this, install the offal of the rural districts as "trustys."

Concerning Punishments, General and Particular, and Their Effects

By A Life Prisoner

From *The Kansas Inferno: A Study of the Criminal Problem; A Description of the Kansas Prison as it is and as it Should Be* by A Life Prisoner (Wichita, Kansas: The Wonderland Publishing Co., 1906).

There are but two logical ways of dealing with a criminal; one is to kill him, the other is to reform him. The first has ever been the popular method among savage tribes; the second is the method of civilization. Punishment has long served the ends of retaliation and revenge, and has even been considered a potent element in effecting reformation. The various forms of bodily torture employed by our ingenious forefathers, such as branding, mutilation, crucifixion, and all manner of cruelties, have given place in comparatively recent times to the practice of punishment by incarceration at hard and unrequited labor. This alteration of methods has changed, but in no degree mitigated, the punishment inflicted on the criminal; for who would not prefer the loss of an ear, or such a matter, to even so much as one year of confinement in a stone sepulcher to be guarded, watched, tortured in body and soul, and lashed by the gaze of the curious.

Additional punishments are inflicted in the Kansas prison for violations of the prison-rules. There are at present four forms of punishment in practice. The least of these consists of depriving the prisoner of his tickets. These tickets are small cards placed in the door of each cell, showing that the occupant has the privilege of drawing books from the library, receiving letters and visits from friends, chewing tobacco, attending the prison-school, and, if he is a Catholic, the privilege of attending mass. When the tickets are removed from the cell-door, the prisoner is deprived of these privileges, and they are not again restored until his punishment is considered of adequate duration.

Another method of punishment is by solitary confinement.

The prisoner is locked in his cell; his tick, pillow, and blankets are removed, leaving him the bare slats of his bunk for a bed; he is allowed no reading-matter; the only food furnished him is a small quantity of bread and water each day; and a close screen is bolted over his door to prevent other prisoners from passing reading-matter or food into his cell. The duration of this punishment may be from five to any number of days fixed by the Deputy Warden.

Punishment in the dark-cell, or "hole," is similar to that of solitary confinement but more severe. The door is boarded up so heavily as to exclude all light and sound, and the cell is absolutely bare, save for a board about thirty inches wide and six and a half feet long, which, as a bed, is but little improvement over the stone Moor. The prisoner is left in absolute silence and darkness, with no company save his own thoughts. After a time he begins to grow hungry, and within four days the hunger has become a gnawing, wolfish agony, which the slight quantity of bread and water only serves to stimulate. No shipwrecked seaman, compelled at last to feast on the bodies of his dead comrades, suffers any more than he. One strong man, whom I saw enter the "hole" to come out thirty-four days later so weak and emaciated that he could not stand or walk without support, told me that when a mouse found its way into the "hole," he made an ineffectual effort to capture it, for he was half insane with hunger; and when at last it escaped him in the darkness, he sat down helplessly and wept and cursed by turns.

On entering the dark-cell, the prisoner is compelled to don a suit of the striped clothing, which as a prison-uniform was abolished some years ago, and must wear it for at least two weeks after his release.

Prisoners are punished on reports of misconduct, which may be made by any of the officers. These reports are recorded under the prisoner's name in a book kept for that purpose. When he applies for a pardon or commutation of sentence, a copy of this record is sent to the Governor, and the reports operate against his release. No record is kept of the temptations conquered, wrong impulses checked, and of the good that he may do—only the evil is recorded; and years of perfect conduct will not obliterate a word.

> *"The moving finger writes; and, having writ,*
> *Moves on: nor all your piety and wit,*
> *Shall lure it back to cancel half a line,*
> *Nor all our tears wash out a word of it."*

If by any chance, one of the numerous officers acquires a personal feeling against the prisoner that officer can easily make his life a hell, and his record as black as ink; for the prisoner is perfectly helpless and, when opposed to the report of an officer, his denials and entreaties count for nothing. The average officer is not of so contemptible a character, but instances of this sort of malicious persecution have occurred, and there is nothing in the present prison-system to prevent their future occurrence. The prisoner should never be punished on a mere accusation, without first having an opportunity to offer a defense before an impartial tribunal of some sort. To punish him unheard is always unreasonable and often unjust.

The punishments just described are the only ones inflicted in the prison that are in harmony with the law regulating the punishments to be administered; and it cannot be denied that they are sufficiently severe to preserve and enforce the most rigid prison-discipline; but there is still another punishment, compared to which these are pleasures. In describing this form of torture, Patrick Lavey, who was for several years a guard at the prison, writes as follows:

"The convict's hands are strapped in a pair of leathern mitts, and a strap is passed through the rings at the wrists and fastened around the waist. Then iron bands are fastened to the muscles of each arm, and another strap is used to draw the arms back to the limit of endurance. In this position the prisoner is thrown into the "crib," the cover is put down and locked with two heavy padlocks, the door of the cell is closed, and the victim is left to suffer and to moan out his misery to the bare stone walls of the empty cell."

The "crib" is a long, trunk-shaped box, constructed of heavy slats, placed some distance apart. There are two of these in present use at the prison. Chains and iron shackles are now used in place of the straps described by Lavey. The prisoner's outer clothing is removed, and he is placed in the "crib" face downward; his hands are fastened together, and his feet are drawn upward and backward until his whole body is stretched taut in the shape of a bow. The intense agony inflicted by this method of torture is indescribable; every muscle of the body quivers and throbs with pain. The punishment is often continued intermittently for days, and sometimes even for weeks. Beating with a heavy strap is usually added, but that is comparatively a small matter.

Section 7052 of the general statutes (1901) of Kansas, relating to the State prison, reads in part as follows:

"THERE SHALL BE NO CORPORAL PUNISHMENT, AND NO PAINFUL AND UNUSUAL KINDS OF PUNISHMENT INFLICTED, SUCH AS BINDING THE LIMBS OR ANY MEMBER THEREOF, OR PLACING OR KEEPING THE PERSON IN A PAINFUL POSTURE."

Here we find manifested a flagrant contempt of law by the prison-officers. Do they hope to cultivate in the prisoner the spirit of law-observance by manifesting in themselves the spirit of lawlessness? These gentlemen are setting a most excellent example to the men and boys who have been placed, bound and helpless, at their mercy, and so placed for that same cause — the violation of law.

If we must revert to barbarism, and debauch the mind and soul of both victim and tormentor with practices belonging to the Dark Ages, then why not remove that humane law from the statute books, and let these satanic cruelties flourish openly and with legal sanction?

Prison Slang

BY JOSEPH "BUNKO" KELLEY

From *Thirteen Years in the Oregon Penitentiary* by Joseph "Bunko" Kelley (Portland, Oregon: N.P., 1908).

Prison slang is made up of many words and phrases which the people outside are not all familiar with. There are "repeaters," "fresh fish," the "head snitch," the "stools," the "stool pigeons," "frame-ups," the "note-writers," the "whisperers," the "men who make the cracks," the "knockers" and the "cons;" sometimes an abbreviation for convict and sometimes meaning a prisoner whose word goes a long way.

The "head snitch" is sometimes called the head flunkey. He is supposed to be the boss over the other flunkeys, but at that he can be a good man. He is supposed to watch the other flunkeys and report them to the chapel guard if he sees any of them doing anything wrong. Very small things are wrong in a penitentiary, that is, under some administrations, where they flog a prisoner for a small thing like asking the head flunkey to get a paper from some cell or some other convict, or to tell any little news he might hear around the prison or from some visitor.

If a screw doesn't "snitch," the guards will throw him into the foundry, so, to hold his job, a man will snitch nine times out of ten. The head snitch had another job until Chamberlain took office. He had to bring the diet of sick men to the cells and if some convict had more tobacco than the sick man he would sell it to him. If the sick man complained to a guard of the fare the head snitch would be called up and he would be asked about it. The head snitch would say, "This man is always kicking about his diet," and the word of the head snitch would be taken in preference to that of the common convict, and the sick man would be chased over to work.

I can speak of the diet from experience. For three months I was on diet which was unsatisfactory until one day Dr. Cusick asked me what I was eating. He had placed me on what they called hospital diet three months before. I was working in the warehouse at the time and was so thin I could scarcely walk to the shops. When the doctor asked me what I was eating I told him the convict grub. The doctor was sitting down at the moment, but when I told him what I had been fed he jumped up and swore.

"I put this man Kelley on diet three months ago," said he to Tom Cornelius, who was deputy warden.

I went to the shops that night. The head snitch came around with a pan of tea and a piece of bread and said: "You don't care about hospital diet." Of course he was put up to make that crack so when he returned to the chapel guard he would be asked, what did Kelley say. And then the head snitch would reply: "He doesn't want that kind of diet." Next the doctor would be told and, of course, the doctor takes the word of the guards. If a man is sick now he is taken to the hospital and is given whatever he can eat. There is a free doctor in attendance, and it is not left to a convict.

Once I lay in my cell twelve days with fever and never ate anything. I had to get out of my bunk and crawl on my hands and knees to the faucet to get a drink of water. J.D. Lee, who was superintendent, knows it. I sent for him one day when I was about all in. He came to the cell to see me and I was informed that the hospital was full. The fact is that I was a lifetimer and they did not want to place me in the hospital.

Two convicts in the next cell saved my life. They had some coffee in their cell and made me a cup. It broke my fever and saved Bunko Kelley's life. If the guard had caught them passing the coffee to me they would have been hung up to the door all night. I will never forget them as long as I live and I hope to meet them some day when I am on Easy street. I hope they will prosper.

The "stool pigeon" is sent around by the guards to hear what the men are saying. If two or more prisoners are seen talking together the stool pigeon butts in and asks the boys how they like the place. Some convict may say to him, "Get away, you stool," and then he runs to the screw and tells that the convict called him a stool. This gets the screw down on that convict, and the prisoner is set down as a bad actor right away. After this, the screw the convict is placed at work under keeps after him and the guard waits for a chance to snare him and hang him up all night at the cell door to take the toughness out of him. Every convict they discover talking to him is informed on by the screw.

When a con knows that a guard wants some stooling done he will hatch up something and get a fellow convict in trouble. I heard a screw tell a prisoner once that if he would do some good stooling the guard would put in a good word for him with the warden and secure some trusty time. The screw told the prisoner, however, that it would have to be very good stooling.

This prisoner, Jim Crow, did good stooling in this manner: He hid some files and nippers and then reported that he saw Jackson, the train-robber, hide them. The screw came running over to the house to see the warden, but it fell through. They were afraid to go ahead with the job, as old Jackson told them he would take off a few of their heads with a hatchet, so they dropped the plot and Jim Crow did not get his good time.

But Crow and his pal would never have thought of doing anything so mean if the guard had not tuned him up to that kind of work. If the guard had bought him a Bible and told the prisoner to read it and when he had read it he would try to secure for the prisoner some good time it would have made a man of the convict instead of a stool pigeon.

When guards teach the prisoners to be villains, what can you expect when they get out of the penitentiary? They will say, "The penitentiary is a snap; we can get in and tell the screws anything and get a soft job and keep out of the shops."

I heard a boy visitor tell his father one day as they came through the shops: "Who is that man asleep up in that chair?" pointing to a guard. A convict heard the remark and dropped a piece of iron on the floor to arouse the screw. The guard jumped down and to pretend that he had not been asleep at his post, said: "Look out, or I will stand you out tonight."

The convict replied that the piece of iron he dropped was not smashed, and when the guard answered, "No back talk," the convict laughed in his sleeve at the joke, and the rest of the prisoners looked wise at the screw. After this the guard went to a stool pigeon and asked how long were the visitors in the shop before he woke up. The stool, wanting to be solid with the guard, replied that the screw had just jumped down as the visitors entered. The guard tried to pass it off by saying that he was just looking down the line at the boys to see that nothing was going wrong.

The guard told the stool to keep his eye on the door and if at any time he saw the super coming to give the screw the "office."

The "frame-up" is a prisoner who tries to get his work in by playing a job. He starts rumors such as one against the food. He will go to fellow prisoners and remark that they had a fine dinner that day, although it may have been nothing but carrots, cabbage, beet tops or boiled spuds. This will cause some convict to remark, "You are trying to frame up something, I guess, to get a pardon." Then the frame-up goes to the commissary and says that the convict is kicking about the good dinner the boys had that day. The commissary will say, "You will make a good man in the kitchen and I will see the warden for you." Thus the frame-up secures a good job. The officers know he will write out a nice letter and boost the dump and do any lying they want him to.

I was badly fooled one day. We had been on the carrot route for about six months when one day Governor Lord came out into the chapel with Manager Gilbert and Brofield. Captain Dickey came out of the kitchen with a convict's pan in his hand heaped up with meat, potatoes, pickles and cabbage. This he showed to Governor Lord.

"That looks pretty good," said the governor. "It ought to be enough for a man."

"Yes," chipped in Brofield, "and they can get more if they want it."

I spread the news that we were going to have a good dinner at last, but when dinner time arrived we had the same old carrots straight and a piece of bone. That was one of their little tricks.

Here is another of their schemes. A number of ladies were visiting the place one afternoon and in going through the cellar they saw a lot of ham and bacon hung up. One woman asked what was done with so much meat. The commissary man answered that it was fed to the convicts. Then one of the good ladies spoke up and said it was better than she gave her family. I would not like to belong to that family, for they must be misers.

"Well," said Captain Dickey to four or five "cellar rats," "take down about ten of them hams and cook them for the boys tonight for supper. They are on their good behavior. And cook plenty of potatoes and cabbage. Give the boys a good blow-out."

A rather good-looking woman asked if they were good hams, and to convince her that they were, Captain Dickey took out his pocket knife and cut off a slice for her to try. The news flew around the prison that the convicts were to have ham for supper, but when supper came there was no ham, nothing but boiled meat and no milk or sugar. After the Good Samaritans went away the hams were hung up again in the same place and Captain Dickey gave the cellar rats the laugh and the convicts blessed Captain Dickey that night.

About a week later another bunch of visitors came to the prison, and one of the women with them had been with the other crowd. When they were looking at the hams, Dickey was making the time-worn talk how they gave the hams to the convicts. The woman who had been in the crowd that visited the place a few days before said:

"Why, Captain, this is the same lot of hams you showed us the other day."

"Oh, they can't be," objected the Captain. "The boys ate them up."

"No," said the woman, "for there is the ham you cut a piece off for me the other day."

Reddening up, Captain Dickey said: "Come along, it's getting late."

But Captain Dickey did not know that the woman had come to the prison the second time just to expose him. It was a put-up job on him. A convict who knew one of the ladies was discharged shortly after the first visit and when he met the woman in Salem and told her of the joke the Captain had played on them, she waited for a chance to expose his trick.

Everyone around Salem who has been there since the penitentiary was established can tell that the talk of the town is that most of the guards that live in that city have smugglers' pockets inside their coats in which to pack off hams, bacon, eggs, butter, lard, beef, chickens and anything else that is eatable. Yet the guards inform visitors that the convicts get these things. Chamberlain put a damper on these doings and now convicts get bacon for dinner sometimes, which they never received under Geer or Lord. I can prove what I am saying and will prove it to anyone who wants to know.

Now for the "knockers." If a convict is trying to get along the best he can the knocker will not let him. The knocker tells some convict whom he thinks stands in with the guards that he heard So and So say the guards are a bad lot and that he would like to kill off a few of them. Perhaps the innocent victim never said a word, but the knocker will go to a convict with a supposed stand-in and will say:

"That fellow who was talking to me says he wants to kill a few guards."

The convict with the pull hunts up a guard and tells the screw what he was told. Of course, the knocker picks out a man that he knows has influence with the guards. He has seen the convict who stands in talking to the guards and giving them little presents, and the man who stands in can come pretty near making the guards think he is telling them the truth.

After hearing the knock, the guards will discuss the proposition and conclude that the knocker is a pretty good fellow and the poor convict that was lied about is getting the worst of it, and he doesn't know where it is coming from. If there was a board of commissioners that the convicts could see there might not be so many breaks from prison, but as it has been in the past, a convict is in a hell hole and could not see anyone.

"Fresh fish" in the penitentiary slang is a man brought to the prison by a sheriff or deputy sheriff and handed over to the turnkey. As soon as the prisoner comes inside and is placed in the receiving cell the head snitch is the only convict permitted to see him. The head snitch is sent by the screws to get his history. In a short time the head snitch brings back the information whether the newcomer is a repeater, an old crook or a Johnny-Come-Lately. This news flies around the prison, and if it is the first offense of the newcomer the cry is "fresh fish, from County So-and-So," "he is a repeater," or whatever the case may be.

All the convicts are singing "fresh fish," and the newcomer imagines he will have fish for breakfast. When the head snitch brings him his pan of beans, the fresh fish may say, "I thought it was fish we were to have for breakfast. I heard everyone saying so."

Then the head snitch explains and observes that if the newcomer kicks about the beans he will get into trouble. The fresh fish is told to take what he gets and say nothing, after which the head snitch slams the wicket. The poor fresh fish sits and thinks he is in bad and waits for the next play to come off, which is when they shear him like a sheep and give him a couple of blankets, and the snitch takes him to a cell. When the new man enters the yard to go over to work he stands alone and is afraid to open his mouth. He looks at the four hundred prisoners while the guards look him over.

The fish is all of a shake and is expecting to be knocked down with a club. He is taken over to the line and one of the screws may hit him in the shins for not keeping up with the other convicts, and if he stops to rub his leg he receives another smash on the back with the stick . When they enter the moulding room he stands there looking at the other convicts working until the free foreman comes over and asks if he has a trade. He may have one, but if he is wise says no, for if he is a moulder, into the moulding room he will go, and he will remain there all his time.

Well the fish is put to work, and the state guard comes along and questions him. The guard says: "Didn't I see you before somewhere? I think you are a second-timer."

"No, sir, I am not," answers the fish.

"Mum is the word here; no talking back," orders the guard. "When you want to speak hold up your hand and come to me, for I am the law here. You have to take your grub and no back slack or I'll fix you every chance I get."

In the penitentiary when a fresh fish arrived he was like an angel from heaven, for that was the only way we could obtain any news from the outside world. That was, however, in the reign of terror under Gilbert and Brofield. Those days are gone now, and while the citizens elect such men as Chamberlain any unfortunate convict can get a square deal.

Slang Among Convicts

By Number 1500

From *Life in Sing Sing* by Number 1500 (Indianapolis: The Bobbs-Merrill Co., 1904).

The use of slang by convicts is very general and is usually for decorative effect rather than for the purpose of concealing from those who may overhear it the meaning of their conversation. It would in fact be valueless for them to use it for that purpose as the guards are as apt with it as the convicts themselves. The possession and management of a large vocabulary of slang is, however, an acquirement of which its possessor is very proud. It is his one literary accomplishment, and he never fails to display and cultivate it at all times.

In listening to a company of prisoners it can be observed that if a new word be spoken whose meaning is only revealed by its context, no sign will be given nor inquiry be made as to its origin or signification. It is simply adopted in silence and assimilated into their speech. In this way the list of slang words is always increasing—the only apparent test of admission being that the word in sound must have some relation to the sense it is intended to convey. But this is perhaps approximately true of all slang. Thieves' slang is very catholic and does not hesitate to accept words from whatever source, so that the field of argot overlaps others. There are, however, many words that are distinctively the possession of the thief and convict, whose use would be applicable to no other condition than his.

I made up a list of these as they came to my notice, and it is perhaps the most complete dictionary of thieves' slang in active service that has ever been made. I have asked professional thieves why they adopted a form of speech which, being overheard by another, would certainly direct suspicion to them, if it did not give rise to active police attention. They replied that its use will not be observed except by those who are "wise" to its meaning, while plain speech could not conceal any part of their communications. Moreover, the efficient use of slang gives the passwords of the profession and are the hailing and recognition signs in its membership.

Stand Pat	Be firm
Thrown Down	Betrayed; deserted
Stood-Out	Reported for infraction of prison rules
Up the River	Sing Sing Prison
Tommy Buster	Woman-beater
Under Cover	Hiding
Wind Jammer	Loquacious person
Turning a Trick	Accomplishing a theft
Whip-Saved	Defeated at all points

Sentences and Translations

A tamaster from Boston	A fugitive from Boston
Are you next?	Do you understand? Be wise
Crushing the jungle	Escaping from prison
Cracking the jug	Forcing an entrance into a bank
Carrying the banner	Walking the streets
Busting the tag on a rattler	Breaking the seal on a freight car
Busting the bulls at the big show	Fighting with the police at the circus
Banging supers at the red wagon	Stealing watches at the ticket wagon
Give him a boost	Speak a good word for him; assist him
Getting the rags from a greaser	Buying counterfeit paper money from an Italian
He sprung the paddy with a screw	He opened the lock with a key
Hitting the pots	Excessive drinking
Holding the mark till the tool whips his stone	Engaging a person's attention till the thief succeeds in stealing his diamond
Hoisting a slab of stones	Stealing a tray of diamonds

He got whipped back to the Irish club house	He was remanded to the police station
He gave them a bull con and they turned him out	He told a plausible story and they discharged him
Hitting the pipe at a hop-joint	Smoking opium in an opium joint
He busted the collar's smeller	He broke the officer's nose
His Tommy has a hoop of stones	His girl has a diamond ring
He got a stretch in the sentence	He got one year in the penitentiary
Rousting a goose for his poke	Jostling a Hebrew so that the pickpocket may steal his purse
The stall got his slats kicked in	The thief had his ribs broken
They clouted him on the kurb and drove him nutty	They struck him on the head, from the effects of which he became insane
The bulls shook him down for their bit	The police compelled them to share the proceeds of the robbery with them
The gun slammed a rod to his nut	The thief put a pistol to his head
He pigged with the darb	He absconded with the money
They threw me down	They deserted me
The yeg men blew the gopher	The safe crackers forced open the doors of the safe with explosives

The tool picked his mark and the stalls crushed him against the tail of the rattler. The gun had just lifted his mitt when the conny fell to the graft and tipped the sucker to the lay. It was a hot foot four hours with the bulls tailing on. It was a clean get-away for mine but for a finger who loved me like a Tommy. His rod to my nut turned me into the Irish Club House. But sin not leary my fall money will spring me down below. No mouth-piece in mine. I've got to be sprung on paper or go to the jungle.

Translation

The pickpocket selected a person to rob. His accomplices crowded him against the backboard of the car. The thief had just raised his hand to begin operating when the conductor suspected him. He warned the victim of his danger and we had to run from the officers who appeared on the scene, but the police pursued. The warm embrace of an officer, accompanied by the pressure of the pistol to the head, turned hope of escape into a certainty of capture, with a trip to the police station. However, I'm not afraid, for the money I have for the purpose will secure my release before my case reaches the upper court. I need no lawyer. I must secure straw bail or go to prison.

I went to the coast with a mob of paper-layers, but graft was on the fritzer. I blew out and rung in with a couple of penny-weighters. A Tommy and his papa. Everything was rosy, the cush was coming strong and I was patting this ginny on the hump, but I was a sooner. The Tommy got a swelled head and we split for all. I did the grand to Chicago and filled in with a yeg mob. We got a country jug on our first touch, but the box wasn't heavy enough for five. They had a plant further on. But we had to wait till one of the mob went for some soup; as I had plenty of the darb I blew away and beat it back to Chic, and framed in with a couple of guns who were working east on the rattlers. We got the stuff all right. Well, I'm off to the joint to smoke-up, so-so.

Translation

I went to California with others to pass worthless checks. There wasn't any money in it, so I left them and went with two expert thieves who make it a practice to rob jewelers, a woman and her lover. Everything looked bright. I was obtaining money easily and I was congratulating myself on my good fortune, but I was too hasty. This woman got independent and we parted for good. I purchased a first-class ticket to Chicago and met a gang of safe burglars whom I joined. Our first theft was the burglary of a safe in a suburban bank. The amount of money obtained was insufficient to repay five men for their trouble. They had in view another place to rob, but we had to wait while one of the men went for some nitroglycerine. As I had plenty of money, I parted from them and returned to Chicago. There I met two pickpockets who were going east on the cars with the intention of plying their trade. We stole a lot of money. And now I'm off to the opium den to smoke some opium. Good-by.

I don't squeal. I had a good run in 'Frisco and I've breathed easy ever since. I can sleep on rocks. I can fall, but no bull could throw me. What! I expand my chest easily? I'm well covered and strong as can be. Oh, yes, I've heard guns shoot, but how were they loaded? You missed the number. They hadn't the shot. Well, we had better unload.

Translation

I don't complain. I was successful while in San Francisco; as a result I have been in comfortable circumstances ever since. I have plenty of money. I can be arrested, but no officer can send me to prison. What, I have unlimited confidence in myself? Why not? I have got enough money and influence to help me out of trouble. Oh, yes, I have heard thieves use the same argument. But you missed the essential point—they lacked the means. Well, we had better alight.

Hello, old man! I'm in for keeps this time. We said that plant and trimmed it nice. But that buster you tipped me to, was a raw one. Everything was on the good, when we got a blow. What does the greaser do but flash his rod and bark away. He plugged the main guy for keeps and I took it on a lam for mine. Plant me for a few moons till the smoke rolls away. It is better to keep under cover while the collars are warm.

Translation

How are you, friend? I mean to stay with you for an indefinite time. We robbed that house and were leaving quietly and well satisfied. But that burglar you introduced to me was a novice. We were discovered—when what does the fellow do but draw his pistol and shoot. He shot and killed the head of the household and I ran away and left him. Hide me for a few months until the affair is forgotten. It is better to stay in hiding while the police are looking for the criminals.

Don't rap. I've been tailed all over the wilds by a mob of western bulls. They had me in Pa, but I ducked them neat. The Pinks are a hard mob to throw, and I'm wise. What's the rap? I don't mind putting you next, for I know you're on the level and won't split. I got a sneak on a jug and it swung heavy, but in making my get-away, the cush got my mug. Pink had me framed and it was like finding rags to the pusher. He picked me right and the bulls were turned loose. They'd have nailed me easy, but the stiffs tipped me to the lay and I've been on the jump since. Hold on! Don't push that gun. What do you mean? I'm pinched. Well, you're a wise guy and I'll have to stand the guff and cave.

Translation

Don't address me; I've been followed all over the country by a number of western detectives. They came very near catching me in Pennsylvania, but I avoided them in time. The Pinkertons are very hard to lose and I know it. What's the charge? I don't mind telling you, for I know you can be trusted. I walked into a bank without attracting the attention of the office force and stole a large sum of money. The cashier saw my face as I fled from the bank and picked my picture from the Rogues' gallery, where Pinkerton placed it some time ago. They would have caught me but for the newspapers printing the story of the robbery and the identity of the thief, and I have been traveling ever since. Stop! Don't shoot! What do you mean? I'm under arrest! Well, you are a clever man and I'll submit to arrest and take the punishment.

One prisoner, who made up most of the list and wrote the sentences illustrative of uses of the words, never except in the company of crooks makes any use of slang at all. His language is not only pure English, but singularly strong and condensed. He is a reader of all sorts of books, a student of politics, an owner of real estate, really in comfortable circumstances, worth perhaps twenty thousand dollars, and yet he is a resolute and capable crook; and although he has done three long terms of imprisonment, has only general ideas about reforming. On being asked why he clung to a business that had so many back-sets, he said that Fred Burnaby, who rode to Kiva, had remarked that after the love season there were only two careers open to a man, war and politics.

"For my own part, neither of these gates was open, although my character and imprisonment need not have barred me from politics in New York City. So I took up the crooked life as furnishing zest and excitement. There are others like me; and it has been observed that many women live in houses of prostitution, not for the profit, but because it is strenuous."

The Dope Habit
By Walter Wilson

From *Hell in Nebraska: A Tale of the Nebraska Penitentiary* by Walter Wilson (Lincoln, Nebraska: The Bankers Publishing Co., 1913).

The most demoralizing, the most degrading of all prison features, is the "dope" habit, which causes endless grief and trouble, not only to the users themselves, but to the prison managers as well. It appears that the use of "dope" originated in England in the seventeenth century when times were hard and wages so low that the people could not afford to indulge in ale or whiskey, but had to find something cheaper, thus started the use of "dope." It was thought with wages rising that this practise would cease but it did not, on the contrary—

> *"Those eat now, who never ate before,*
> *And those who always ate, now eat the more"*

and from England the habit spread all over the world, and once a slave of this deadly drug it is almost impossible to dispense with it. To get it, a user will lie, steal, even commit murder, and under the influence of it he will commit any crime on the calendar. Many prisoners are users of "dope" when they come to the prison, and try to smuggle a supply in with them in various ways, mostly in their shoes. I have seen the heels of a pair of shoes hollowed out and sufficient "dope" inserted to last a man for several years. Of course this is promptly destroyed. Some of the prisoners who never used it on the outside become users of it in prison. Perhaps they are put in the cell with one of these "dope" fiends who invites them to try it. They do, and like it. Soon they take another jolt and before they know it, they become "dope" fiends themselves.

There is, however, some excuse for prisoners using this poison. Some of them, having been behind the bars for many years, completely shut off from all stimulants, after years of hard work, and all the time doing over and over again the same monotonous prison routine, find themselves some day mentally and physically weak and in need of some stimulant, and not being able to get any liquors, resort to "dope." Others may be sick, or have some grievance, imaginary or otherwise, and try to drown their troubles by using "dope." Looking at it in this light, there may be some excuse for it; and if you, my reader, were lying in a little steel cell in deadly pain or worried to death over the turn your affairs had taken, and sleep would not come to you, if one little piece of morphine about the size of a pinhead would put you to sleep, and give you sweet dreams besides, many of you would fall for it. Dreams of the sweetest kind come to the users of "dope," pipe dreams as they are commonly called; perhaps you see the pearly gates and the garden of paradise and the house of many mansions. I recall the poet's description of such a pipe dream:

> "The appearance instantaneously disclosed
> Was of a mighty city—boldly say
> A wilderness of building, sinking far
> And self withdrawn into a wondrous depth
> Far sinking into splendor without end,
> Fabric it seemed of diamond and of gold
> With alabaster domes and silver spires
> And blazing terrace upon terrace, high
> Uplifted, here serene pavillions bright
> In avenues disposed, there towers begirt
> With battlements that on their restless fronts
> Bore stars—illuminations of all gems."

What an awful disappointment after dreaming such a dream, to awaken and find yourself behind the prison bars. And after the awakening comes those awful pains for which there is but one cure—another jolt of "dope." Much attention has been paid to an article read by Judge Lincoln Frost before the Social Service Club, dealing with the "dope" habit and other vices at the penitentiary. Before completing this chapter I called upon the judge. I asked him if he had ever met Mr. Delahunty, and he said that he did not even know him personally. I told him that I wished that he had called upon the warden and gotten the information from him. There being always two sides to a story, it is well to hear both sides; and if Judge Frost had gone in person to the prison and called upon the warden, I am certain that several errors that appear in his paper would not have appeared there. For a fact one of the inmates who furnished him with much information, especially against the inmate physician, Mr. Dinsmore, admitted to the judge that he had himself sold "dope" at the pen. No matter what Mr. Dinsmore has done behind the prison bars, no matter what crime he committed to go there, give him his dues; and if those who abuse him could have seen what I saw, when the prison officials lay wounded how tenderly they were cared for by Mr. Dinsmore—those people would themselves, if possessed of a heart at all, suggest that he be pardoned. While it is true that he is not a graduate physician, we must remember that the great state pays its doctor only seventy-five dollars and for that little amount he cannot spend all his time at the prison. Rather than to let a man injured in the factory bleed to death, is it not better to have him attended to by one who understands how, even if he does not possess a diploma? The story of him administering poison to another inmate is too absurd to comment upon.

It is indeed surprising how the "dope" is smuggled into the prison. Some was concealed in the coal cars and a chalk mark made on the car. Once a negro woman left some English walnuts, which we opened and found filled with "dope" and carefully pasted together. Another time a woman brought several sacks of smoking tobacco, on which the revenue stamps had been carefully removed, "dope" inserted, and then carefully sealed again. Warden Melick had this woman arrested and she served a sentence in the county jail. But to thoroughly and completely eradicate this evil, you must have the law with you, and at Warden Melick's suggestion, a law was enacted making it a felony for bringing "dope" and liquor into the prison and thus far no one has been willing to take such chances. What a pity that this law was not passed many years ago.

On a cold winter night Judge Frost, Rev. Roach, Bert Wilson and a Mr. McBride together with two ex-convicts bent upon revenge, went to the prison on the ten o'clock car, went to the wooden gate, called a trusty and handed to him a bottle of morphine—enough to kill several men. It was indeed a nice affair for a former circuit judge to take part in. I am sorry that all of these gentlemen were not nabbed and jailed which they should have been, two of them committing a crime and the other four witnessing it. Was it a wonder that such a judge was retired to obscurity? Rev. Roach has also been noted as a man attending more to other peoples' affairs than to his own. Bert Wilson is the man who furnished a traveling evangelist with much information that helped the city to go wet instead of going dry; and Mr. McBride—well, his lyceum fame and obtaining thousands of dollars is well known to the public. He succeeded in catching several prominent men for sums ranging from fifty to two hundred dollars and then his lyceum bureau went under. Had he not better sweep before his own door and let his neighbor alone?

Prostitution in the Pen

> *"Who keeps the mastery of himself!*
> *If one Ponders on objects of the sense, there springs*
> *Attraction: from attraction grows desire*
> *Desire flames to fierce passion, passion breeds*
> *Recklessness: then the memory—all betrayed—*
> *Lets noble purpose go, and saps the mind,*
> *Till purpose, mind, and man are all undone."*

Those of my readers who are so good, so modest, had better skip this chapter, for it speaks about prostitution. "What do you mean," asks my reader, "are not the two sexes segregated at the prison?" Yes, they are, the men being in one building and the women in another, and the two do never mingle. The prostitution that exists is that which is practised by men among men or by men to boys. To make it any plainer would perhaps land me in the federal prison for many years, for it is unfit to print and transmit through the mails. That my reader shall understand the situation, I will say "Get your Bible and read the first chapter of St. Pauls' letter to the Romans, especially the 26th and 27th verses, which read as follows: 26. For this cause God gave them up unto vile affections; for even their women did change the natural use into that which is against nature. 27. And likewise also the men leaving the natural use of the woman, burned in their lust one toward another; men with men working that which is unseemly, and receiving in themselves that recompense of their error which was meet.

Never did I imagine that a human being could thus lower himself, and if those old steel cells at Lancaster or in any other prison for that matter could speak, they would reveal crimes like those Saint Paul writes about, crimes almost unbelievable, practised by old offenders, serving long sentences and being shut off from the opposite sex forever, upon the young inmates, crimes so black that they would make the "hangers on" of an oriental seraglio blush with shame. A young man thus ravished is ruined forever. "How can it be prevented?" you ask. There are two ways: first, you parents, guide and look after your boys and keep them out of the penitentiary; second, segregate those unfortunate boys who have to go there from the old sodomists by erecting reformatories for these young men, where the individual boy can be watched and the individual case receive that particular treatment which is most necessary. Warden Melick speaks of this in his report, and Governor Aldrich in his message asked the legislators to appropriate funds for such a reformatory, which they did, and soon our state is to have such an institution.

In Stir

By Light-Fingered Jim

From *The Autobiography of a Thief,* Recorded by Hutchins Hapgood
(New York: Fox, Duffield & Co., 1903).

I hung my head with shame, but not because of contrition. I
was ashamed of being caught and made a spectacle of. All the
way to Sing Sing station people stared at us as if we were wild
animals. We walked from the town to the prison, in close company with two deputy sheriffs. I observed considerably, knowing that I should not see the outside world again for a number
of years. I looked with envy at the people we passed who
seemed honest, and thought of home and the chances I had
thrown away.

When I reached the stir I was put through the usual cere-
monies. My pedigree was taken, but I told the examiners nothing. I gave them a false name and a false pedigree. Then a bath
was given to my clothes and I was taken to the tailor shop.
When my hair had been cropped close and a suit of stripes given
me I felt what it was to be the convicted criminal. It was not a
pleasant feeling, I can tell you, and when I was taken to my cell
my heart sank indeed. A narrow room, seven feet, four inches
long; dark, damp, with moisture on the walls, and an old iron
cot with plenty of company, as I afterwards discovered—this
was to be my home for years. And I as full of life as a young
goat! How could I bear it?

After I had been examined by the doctor and questioned
about my religion by the chaplain, I was left to reflect in my
cell. I was interrupted in my melancholy train of thought by
two convicts who were at work in the hall just outside my cell.
I had known them on the outside, and they, taking good care
not to be seen by the screws (keepers), tipped me off through
my prison door to everything in stir which was necessary for a
first timer to know. They told me to keep my mouth shut, to
take everything from the screws in silence, and if assigned to a
shop to do my work. They told me who the stool-pigeons were,

that is to say, the convicts who, in order to curry favor and have an easy time, put the keepers next to what other convicts are doing, and so help to prevent escapes. They tipped me off to those keepers who were hard to get along with, and put me next to the Underground Tunnel, and who were running it. Sing Sing, they said, is the best of the three New York penitentiaries: for the grub is better than at the others, there are more privileges, and, above all, it is nearer New York, so that your friends can visit you more frequently. They gave me a good deal of prison gossip, and told me who among my friends were there, and what their condition of health was. So and so had died or gone home, they said, such and such had been drafted to Auburn or Clinton prisons. If I wanted to communicate with my friends in stir all that was necessary for me to do was to write a few stiffs (letters) and they would be sent by the Underground Tunnel. They asked me about their old pals, hangouts and girls in New York, and I, in turn, gave them a lot of New York gossip. Like all convicts they shed a part of the things they had received from home, gave me canned goods, tobacco and a pipe. It did not take me long to get on to the workings of the prison.

I was particularly interested in the Underground Tunnel, for I saw at once its usefulness. This is the secret system by which contraband articles, such as whiskey, opium and morphine are brought into the prison. When a rogue is persuasive with the coin of the realm he can always find a keeper or two to bring him what he considers the necessaries of life, among which are opium, whiskey and tobacco. If you have a screw "right," you can be well supplied with these little things. To get him "right" it is often necessary to give him a share—about twenty per cent—of the money sent you from home. This system is worked in all the State prisons in New York, and during my first term, or any of the other terms for that matter, I had no difficulty in supplying my growing need for opium.

I do not want people to get the idea that it is always necessary to bribe a keeper in order to obtain these little luxuries; for many a screw has brought me whiskey and hop, and con-

traband letters from other inmates, without demanding a penny.
A keeper is a human being like the rest of us, and he is sometimes moved by considerations other than of pelf. No matter
how good and conscientious he may be, a keeper is but a man
after all, and, having very little to do, especially if he is in
charge of an idle gang of "cons" he is apt to enter into conversation with them, particularly if they are better educated or
more interesting than he, which often is the case. They tell him
about their escapades on the outside and often get his sympathy and friendship. It is only natural that those keepers who are
good fellows should do small favors for certain convicts. They
may begin by bringing the convicts newspapers to read, but
they will end by providing them with almost everything. Some
of them, however, are so lacking in human sympathy that their
kindness is aroused only by a glimpse of the coin of the realm;
or by the prospect of getting some convict to do their dirty
work for them, that is, to spy upon their fellow prisoners.

At Auburn penitentiary, whither I was drafted after nine
months at Sing Sing, a few of the convicts peddled opium and
whiskey, with, of course, the connivance of the keepers. There
are always some persons in prison as well as out who want to
make capital out of the misfortunes of others. These peddlars
were despised by the rest of the convicts, for they were invariably stool-pigeons; and young convicts who never before knew
the power of the drug became opium fiends, all on account of
the business propensities of these detestable rats (stool-pigeons)
who, because they had money and kept the screws next to those
cons who tried to escape, lived in Easy Street while in stir.

While on this subject, I will tell about a certain famous
"fence" (at one of these prisons) although he did not operate
until my second term. At that time things were booming on
the outside. The graft was so good that certain convicts in my
clique were getting good dough sent them by their pals who
were at liberty; and many luxuries came in, therefore, by the
Underground Tunnel. Now those keepers who are next to the
Underground develop, through their association with convicts,
a propensity to graft, but usually have not the nerve to hustle

for the goods. So they are willing to accept stolen property, not having the courage and skill to steal, from the inhabitants of the under world. A convict, whom I knew when at liberty, named Mike, thought he saw an opportunity to do a good "fencing" business in prison. He gave a "red-front" (gold watch and chain), which he had stolen in his good days, to a certain keeper who was running the Underground, and thus got him "right." Then Mike made arrangements with two grafters on the outside to supply the keeper and his friends with what they wanted. If the keeper said his girl wanted a stone, Mike would send word to one of the thieves on the outside to supply a good diamond as quickly as possible. The keeper would give Mike a fair price for these valuable articles and then sell the stones or watches, or make his girl a present.

Other keepers followed suit, for they couldn't see how there was any "come-back" possible, and soon Mike was doing a thriving business. It lasted for five or six months, when Mike stopped it as a regular graft because of the growing cupidity of the keepers. One of them ordered a woman's watch and chain and a pair of diamond ear-rings through the Underground Tunnel. Mike obtained the required articles, but the keeper paid only half of what he promised, and Mike thereupon shut up shop. Occasionally, however, he continued to sell goods stolen by his pals who were at liberty, but only for cash on the spot, and refused all credit. The keepers gradually got a great feeling of respect for this convict "fence" who was so clever and who stood up for his rights; and the business went on smoothly again, for a while.

But finally it was broken up for good. A grafter on the outside, Tommy, sent through the Underground a pawn ticket for some valuable goods, among them a sealskin sacque worth three hundred dollars, which he had stolen and hocked in Philadelphia. Mike sold the pawn-ticket to a screw. Soon after that Tommy, or one of his pals, got a fall and "squealed." The police got "next" to where the goods were, and when the keeper sent the ticket and the money to redeem the articles they allowed them to be forwarded to the prison, but arrested the keeper for receiving stolen goods. He was convicted and sentenced to ten years, but got off through influence. That, however, finished the "fence" at the institution.

To resume the thread of my narrative, the day after I reached Sing Sing I was put through the routine that lasted all the time I was there. At six-thirty in the morning we were awakened by the bell and marched in lock-step (from which many of us were to acquire a peculiar gait that was to mark us through life and help prevent us from leading decent lives) to the bucket-shop, where we washed, marched to the mess for breakfast at seven-thirty, then to the various shops to work until eleven-thirty, when at the whistle we would form again into squads and march, again in the lock-step, fraternally but silently, to our solemn dinner, which we ate in dead silence. Silence, indeed, except on the sly, was the general rule of our day, until work was over, when we could whisper together until five o'-clock, the hour to return to our cells, into which we would carry bread for supper, coffee being conveyed to us through a spout in the wall. The food at Sing Sing was pretty good. Breakfast consisted of hash or molasses, black coffee and bread; and at dinner we had pork and beans, potatoes, hot coffee and bread. Pork and beans gave place to four eggs on Friday, and sometimes stews were given us. It was true what I'd heard, that Sing Sing has the best food of any institution I have known. After five o'clock I would read in my cell by an oil lamp (since my time electricity has been put in the prison) until nine o'clock, when I had to put out my light and go to bed.

I had a great deal more time for reading and meditation in my lonely cell than one would think by the above routine. I was put to work in the shop making chairs. It was the first time I had ever worked in my life, and I took my time about it. I felt no strong desire to work for the State. I was expected to cane a hundred chairs a day, but I usually caned about two. I did not believe in work. I felt at that time that New York State owed me a living. I was getting a living all right, but I was ungrateful. I did not thank them a wee bit. I must have been a bad example to other " cons," for they began to get as tired as myself. At any rate, I lost my job, and was sent back to my cell, where I stayed most of the time while at Sing Sing.

I worked, indeed, very little at any time during my three bits in the penitentiary. The prison at Sing Sing, during the nine months I was there on my first term, was very crowded, and there was not enough work to go round; and I was absolutely idle most of the time. When I had been drafted to Auburn I found more work to do, but still very little, for it was just then that the legislature had shut down on contract labor in the prisons. The outside merchants squealed because they could not compete with unpaid convict labor; and so the prison authorities had to shut down many of their shops, running only enough to supply the inside demand, which was slight. For eighteen months at Auburn I did not work a day. I think it was a very bad thing for the health of convicts when this law was passed; for certainly idleness is a very bad thing for most of them; and to be shut up nearly all the time in damp, unhealthy cells like those at Sing Sing is a terrible strain on the human system.

Personally, however, I liked to be in my cell, especially during my first year of solitary confinement, before my health began to give way; for I had my books from the good prison libraries, my pipe or cigarettes, and last, but not least, I had a certain portion of opium that I used every day.

For me, prison life had one great advantage. It broke down my health and confirmed me for many years in the opium habit; but I educated myself while in stir. Previous to going to Sing Sing my education had been almost entirely in the line of graft; but in stir, I read the English classics and became familiar with philosophy and the science of medicine and learned something about chemistry.

One of my favorite authors was Voltaire, whom I read, of course, in a translation. His "Dictionary" was contraband in prison but I read it with profit. Voltaire was certainly one of the shrewdest of men, and as up to snuff as any cynical grafter I know, and yet he had a great love for humanity. He was the philosopher of humanity. Goethe said that Luther threw the world back two hundred years, but I deny it; for Luther, like Voltaire, pointed out the ignorance and wickedness of the priests of their day. These churchmen did not understand the teachings of Christ. Was Voltaire delusional? The priests must have thought so, but they were no judges, for they were far worse and less humane than the French revolutionists. The latter killed outright, but the priests tortured in the name of the Most Humane. I never approved of the methods of the French revolutionists, but certainly they were gentle in comparison with the priests of the Spanish Inquisition.

I think that, in variety of subjects, Voltaire has no equal among writers. Shrewd as he was, he had a soul, and his moral courage was grand. His defense of young Barry, who was arrested for using language against the church, showed his kindness and breadth of mind. On his arrival in Paris, when he was only a stripling, he denounced the cowardly, fawning sycophants who surrounded Louis XIV [sic], and wrote a sarcastic poem on His Nibs, and was confined in the Bastille for two years. His courage, his wit, his sarcasms, his hatred of his persecutors, and his love and kindness, stamp him as one of the great, healthy intellects of mankind. What a clever book is *Candide!* What satire! What wit! As I lay on my cot how often I laughed at his caustic comments on humanity! And how he could hate! I never yet met a man of any account who was not a good hater. I own that Voltaire was ungallant toward the fair sex. But that was his only fault.

I enjoyed Victor Hugo because he could create a great character, and was capable of writing a story with a plot. I rank him as a master of fiction, although I preferred his experience as a traveller to his novels, which are not real enough. Ernest Renan was a bracing and clever writer, but I was sadly disappointed in reading his *Life of Jesus.* I expected to get a true outline of Christ's time and a character sketch of the man himself, but I didn't. I went to the fountain for a glass of good wine, but got only red lemonade.

I liked Dumas, and revelled in the series beginning with *The Three Musketeers.* I could not read Dumas now, however. I also enjoyed Gaboriau and Du Boisgobey, for they are very sensational; but that was during my first term in stir. I could not turn a page of their books now, for they would seem idiotic to me. Balzac is a bird of another feather. In my opinion he was one of the best dissectors of human nature that the world ever produced. Not even Shakespeare was his equal. His depth in searching for motives, his discernment in detecting a hypocrite, his skill in showing up women with their follies, their loves, their little hypocrisies, their endearments, their malice and their envy is unrivalled. It is right that Balzac should show woman with all her faults and follies and virtues, for if she did not possess all these characteristics, how could man adore her?

In his line I think Thackeray is as great as Balzac. When I had read *Vanity Fair, Pendennis, The Newcomes,* and *Barry Lyndon,* I was so much interested that I read anything of his I could lay my hands on, over and over again. With a novel of Thackeray's in my hand I would become oblivious to my surroundings, and long to know something of this writer's personality. I think I formed his mental make-up correctly, for I imagined him to be gentle and humane. Any man with ability and brains equal to his could not be otherwise. What a character is Becky Sharp! In her way she was as clever a grafter as Sheenie Annie. She did not love Rawdon as a good wife should. If she had she would not be the interesting Becky that she is. She was grateful to Rawdon for three reasons; first, he married her; second, he gave her a glimpse into a station in life her soul longed for; third, he came from a good family, and was a soldier and tall, and it is well-known that little women like big men. Then Rawdon amused Becky. She often grinned at his lack of brains. She grinned at everything, and when we learn that Becky got religion at the end of the book, instead of saying, God bless her, we only grin, too.

Pendennis is a healthy book. I always sympathize with Pen and Laura in their struggles to get on, and when the baby was born I was willing to become Godpapa, just for its Mamma's sake. *The Newcomes* I call Thackeray's masterpiece. It is truer to life than any other book I ever read. Take the scene where young Clive throws the glass of wine in his cousin's face. The honest horror of the father, his indignation when old Captain Costigan uses bad language, his exit when he hears a song in the Music Hall—all this is true realism. But the scene that makes this book Thackeray's masterpiece is that where the old Colonel is dying. The touching devotion of Madam and Ethel, the love for old Tom, his last word *"adsum,"* the quiet weeping of his nurse, and the last duties to the dead; the beautiful tenderness of the two women, of a kind that makes the fair sex respected by all men—I can never forget this scene till my dying day.

When I was sick in stir a better tonic than the quack could prescribe was Thackeray's *Book of Snobs.* Many is the night I could not sleep until I had read this book with a relish. It acted on me like a bottle of good wine, leaving me peaceful after a time of pleasure. In this book are shown up the little egotisms of the goslings and the foibles of the sucklings in a masterly manner.

I read every word Dickens ever wrote; and I often ruminated in my mind as to which of his works is the masterpiece. *Our Mutual Friend* is weak in the love scenes, but the book is made readable by two characters, Noddy Boffin and Silas Wegg. Where Wegg reads, as he thinks, *The Last of the Russians,* when the book was *The Decline and Fall of the Roman Empire,* there is the quintessence of humor. Silas's wooden leg and his occupation of selling eggs would make anybody smile, even a dip who had fallen and had no money to square it.

The greatest character in *David Copperfield* is Uriah Heep. The prison scene where this humble hypocrite showed he knew his Bible thoroughly, and knew the advantage of having some holy quotations pat, reminded me often of men I have known in Auburn and Sing Sing prisons. Some hypocritical jailbird would dream that he could succeed on the outside by becoming a Sunday School superintendent; and four of the meanest thieves I ever knew got their start in that way. Who has not enjoyed Micawber, with his frothy personality and straitened circumstances, and the unctious Barkis—Poor Emily! Who could blame her? What woman could help liking Steerforth?

Part Three: Life Behind the Bars

It is strange and true that good women are won by men they know to be rascals. Is it the contrast between Good and Evil, or is it because the ne'er-do-well has a stronger character and more magnetic force? Agnes was one of the best women in the world. Contrast her with David's first wife. Agnes was like a fine violin, while Dora was like a wailing hurdy-gurdy.

Oliver Twist is Dickens's strongest book. He goes deeper into human nature there than in any other of his writings. Fagin, the Jew, is a very strong character, but overdrawn. The picture of Fagin's dens and of the people in them is true to life. I have seen similar gatherings many a time. The ramblings of the Artful Dodger are drawn from the real thing, but I never met in real life such a brutal character as Bill Sykes; and I have met some tough grafters, as the course of this book will show. Nancy Sykes, however, is true to life. In her degradation she was still a woman. I contend that a woman is never so low but a man was the cause. One passage in the book has often touched me, as it showed that Nancy had not lost her sex. When she and Bill were passing the prison, she turned towards it and said: "Bill, they were fine fellows that died to-day." "Shut your mouth," said Bill. Now I don't think there is a thief in the United States who would have answered Nancy's remark that way. Strong arm workers who would beat your brains out for a few dollars would be moved by that touch of pity in Nancy's voice.

But Oliver himself is the great character, and his story reminds me of my own. The touching incident in the work-house where his poor stomach is not full, and he asks for a second platter of mush to the horror of the teachers, is not overdrawn. When I was in one of our penal institutions, at a later time of my life, I was ill, and asked for extra food; but my request was looked upon as the audacity of a hardened villain. I had many such opportunities to think of Oliver.

I always liked those authors who wrote as near life as decency would permit. Sterne's *Tristam Shandy* has often amused me, and *Tom Jones, Roderick Random* and *Peregrine Pickle* I have read over and over again. I don't see why good people object to such books. Some people are forever looking after the affairs of others and neglecting their own; especially a man whom I will call Common Socks who has put himself up as a mentor for over seventy millions of people. Let me tell the busy ladies who are afraid that such books will harm the morals of young persons that the more they are cried down the more they will be read. For that matter they ought to be read. Why object to the girl of sixteen reading such books and not to the woman of thirty-five? I think their mental strength is about equal. Both are romantic and the woman of thirty-five will fall in love as quickly as the girl of sixteen. I think a woman is always a girl; at least, it has been so in my experience. One day I was grafting in Philadelphia. It was raining, and a woman was walking along on Walnut Street. She slipped on the wet sidewalk and fell. I ran to her assistance, and saw that her figure was slim and girlish and that she had a round, rosy face, but that her hair was pure white. When I asked her if she was hurt, she said "yes," but when I said "Let me be your grandson and support you on my way," I put my foot into it, for, horrors! the look she gave me, as she said in an icy voice, "I was never married!" I wondered what manner of men there were in Philadelphia, and, to square myself, I said: "Never married! and with a pair of such pretty ankles!" Then she gave me a look, thanked me, and walked away as jauntily as she ever did in her life, though she must have been suffering agonies from her sprained ankle. Since that time I have been convinced that they of the gentle sex are girls from fifteen to eighty.

I read much of Lever, too, while I was in stir. His pictures of Ireland and of the noisy strife in Parliament, the description of Dublin with its spendthrifts and excited populace, the gamblers and the ruined but gay young gentlemen, all mixed up with the grandeur of Ireland, are the work of a master. I could only compare this epoch of worn-out regalia with a St. Patrick's day parade twenty years ago in the fourth ward of Manhattan.

Other books I read in stir were Gibbon's *Roman Empire,* Carlyle's *Frederick the Great,* and many of the English poets. I read Wordsworth, Gray and Goldsmith, but I liked Tom

Moore and Robert Burns better. The greatest of all the poets, however, in my estimation, is Byron. His loves were many, his adventures daring, and his language was as broad and independent as his mind.

Literary Convicts
By a Newspaper Reporter

From *The Prisoners of the Ohio Penitentiary; the Daily Routine of Their Lives, What They are Compelled to Do, the System of Their Government, Their Punishments, etc. With Stories of Memorable Escapes, and the Remarkable Histories of Noted Convicts* by a Newspaper Reporter (Columbus, Ohio: Hann & Adair, 1883).

Criminals are by no means all poor in the degree of the cultivation of their minds, and many possess a superior order of intelligence which, if bent in honorable directions, would make them prominent and honored citizens. In the loneliness of their cells they have much to think about, and while some study plans for mischief, to be put into execution upon their release, many turn their attention to the acquisition of useful knowledge. Recently a man who has many years yet to serve behind the bars requested a text book on higher mathematics, and it was sent to him by Mr. R.W. Stevenson, Superintendent of the Public Schools of Columbus, with an encouraging inscription. He is now acquiring knowledge which will be of value to him when he comes into the world again, and at the same time occupying his mind in a healthy way, which affords him great pleasure and enables him to enjoy existence again. In the prison library is a large number of the works of the best writers, and hundreds of convicts read these at nights with the liveliest enjoyment. Others make a special study of religious topics, and profess conversion. In the Chapel "experience meetings" convicts speak in public in a way which shows them to be of very good literary powers. Of course these men are few compared with the whole number incarcerated.

Poetry is frequently written by the prisoners and many of their verses have found their way into the newspapers and magazines on account of their excellence. Those given here, however, were received from the writers themselves, and have never before appeared in print. Only a few are given, selections from a large number at hand, to show the character of the whole.

The following sad verses were written by a life convict, and are interesting as reflecting the thoughts and feelings of a man in the extraordinary circumstances described. The convict C.M. Turner is imprisoned under the name of Alonzo Neeley, No. 11,063. He was sent from Allen county, being received March 13, 1876. His offense was a brutal assault upon a nine-year-old girl, the first convicted under the law making that crime punishable by life imprisonment. Application has been made for his pardon. The verses are as follows:

A Prisoner for Life

Alonzo Neeley, a prisoner for life,
 Deserted by friends, by father and wife,
 Left to his fate and his dark, dreary cell,
 To the world and its joys he has bidden farewell.

As he lay in his cell one dark, gloomy night,
 And thought of the past, and time's weary flight,
 Of the long, weary years he had been a poor slave,
 No liberty for him this side of the grave,

As he lay in deep thought on his hard, narrow bed,
 And thought of his fate, all hope from him fled.
 He cried: "Oh, God! is this surely my doom!
 Is there no one to save me from this living tomb?

Never again shall I roam the green earth,
 Never again see the land of my birth,
 The woodland and meadow, the home of my childhood,
 The bright, rolling river or the cool shady wildwood.

The hopes of my youth and manhood have perished,
 All gone with the friends that once I so cherished.

Must I languish and die and a felon's grave fill?
Oh, God, I submit if this be thy will."
The hours passed on, the prisoner slept,
On his cheek was the tear he had bitterly wept;
But now in his slumber he has forgotten his sorrow,
 Sleep on, prison slave, till the light of to-morrow,

As he slept he dreamed of his childhood hours,
Of the old farm-house, of the garden and flowers,
Of the orchard and meadow, of the trees on the hill,
Of the church and the school-house, the brook and the mill.

Again in his childhood, by his mother he stood.
 Her countenance seemed radiant, beautiful and good.
She seemed to be one of a beautiful throng,
They sang low, sweet music; 'twas a bright angel song.

Again, in his dream, he stood a tall youth,
He had left the pathway of temperance and truth;
He leaned 'gainst the bar of the village inn,
He swallowed that poison—his first glass of gin.

His companions were youths, like him, gone astray,
They seemed so light-hearted, buoyant and gay;
They emptied their glasses, then joined in a song.
'Twas loud and discordant, like the sound of a gong.

The vision is ended. The dreamer awoke,
At length in low, trembling accents he spoke:
"Oh, that sound has awakened me; I know it well,
'Tis the horrible clang of the Deputy's bell."

Yes, that bell is the signal that the day has begun,
How many hearts tremble at its terrible clang,
It calls us poor slaves to one more day of sorrow,
 Yet many look forward with hope to the morrow!

One would hardly expect heroic and patriotic sentiments in a horse thief, but here is a poem which compares favorably with many which have a place in literature, written by a man convicted of horse stealing in Cincinnati. It was composed in spare moments which he could steal from his work of looking after the patterns in use on the Patton Manufacturing Company's contract:

WAVE ON, BRIGHT BANNER!

Decoration Ode

To the American Flag, erected over the graves of our fallen heroes

By Thomas H. Thomas

Wave on, Bright Banner, wave!
A thousand heroes brave
    Sleep 'neath thy fold.
A nation's crimson flood
 Of consecrated blood
Where once the traitor stood
    For thee hath rolled!

Wave on, Bright Banner, wave!
O'er those whose life-blood gave
    Thy stars new pride
Our country boasts each name
At whose first call they came
And there, midst battle's flame,
    So nobly died!

Wave on, Fair Banner, wave!
The arms which struck to save
    Are low in death!
Now thou dost guard their tomb
Where traitors, bowed in gloom,

Oft pass and curse their doom
   In sullen breath!

Wave on, Soft Banner, wave,
Sweet guardian o'er the grave
   Of those who fell!
When treason's mighty hand
Spread gloom throughout the land,
In front they took their stand
   Foes to repel.

Wave on, Sweet Banner, wave!
A land that owns no slave
   Is now thy boast.
May the stripes ever be
Emblem of all that's free
Till every nation see
   And love thee most!

—A Female Poet

On the 30th of April, 1883, there was discharged by expiration of sentence, a young woman incarcerated under the name of Nellie Hardy. She was born of excellent parents in England, and liberally educated. Graduating early in life from one of the most eminent seminaries for ladies in the mother country, she came to America and engaged in literary work. At one time she occupied a place of some prominence as a temperance lecturer. She was married and formed a most unfortunate habit of drinking. It rapidly grew upon her and she was soon degraded to a fearful extent. She married again while yet bound to her first husband, and for this crime was sent to the Ohio Penitentiary. Her drinking habit had so lowered her self-respect that, though very fair and highly intelligent, she consorted with a low negro, a sailor on Lake Erie. In prison she was universally liked. She was very bright and sprightly, notwithstanding her imprisonment, and, with the poison which had been her curse removed, she was extremely ladylike, and seemed strangely out of place behind the bars. When she departed from the prison she left a copy book filled with a large number of original short poems and a few prose pieces, written upon various topics, which she called "scribbling by Nellie Hardy." Some of the poems possess literary excellence, but the following is copied more to show the nature and hopes of the woman convict:

Link by link I forged the chain
    That binds me now,
Promise upon promise broken
    Vain each vow.

Grain by grain I sowed the seed
    That has now taken root,
And to the sower brought
    Such bitter fruit.

Drop by drop with my own hands,
    I filled the cup
That, to the very dregs, my God
    Has given me to sup.

And from my heart I cry, "oh Lord,
    How long will this yet last?"
But vain oh vain, is each request,
    I cannot undo the past.

But in future—who will tell,
    I have a future still,
Fresh seed to sow, new chains to forge,
    So bend to heavens will.

And on the chain I forge, the seed I sow,
    Oh Lord, a blessing pray bestow.

—A Love-Sick Prisoner

The woman had a tender passion for a man in stripes whom she designated by the name of "A.E." In her collection of poems she wrote one inscribed, "To A.E., Beloved by me." It is as follows:

Prison and prison life
    Are very hard to bear,
And harder still when those we love
    In those hardships have a share.

And now I long for Sunday—for—
    (Though I love the service too)
Sunday I love the best because I get a glimpse of you.

Some may think it foolishness,
    But, oh, they cannot tell
How dear it is to the loving heart
    Of your little loving Nell—

Only a momentary glance,
    A passing glimpse of you,
Yet dear to me as to the earth
    Are early drops of dew.

Cheer up, dear one, for oh, I trust,
    When these dark days pass by,
On earth there'll be no happier pair
    Than Aleck E—and I.

For out of wintry darkness
    The summer sun will shine,
And our hears will beam with brightness
When I am yours and you are mine.

Here is one which she wrote to Coy Hardy, "who promised money in seven letters and failed to send it":

Eucher

Never mind, it is a point or two
More than I have ever scored 'gainst you,
And if you play, however hard,
Still I hold the winning card.
Another trick or two pray try,
When "eucher" you'll be glad to cry.
You may think yours is a quiet game,
But, dear old boy, I play the same.
I'll own, your playing is first-class,
But my hand's full. Go on, I pass.

Another to the same person. He is the negro husband before referred to:

A Poetic Plea for Money

If you loved me—loved me true—
You'd write more often than you do.
But out of sight and out of mind,
Is true in your case, too, I find.
Never fear, the time will come—
I'll say the rest when I come home.
But one thing I will say to you,
Send me, dear, a dollar or two.
If I do not receive it soon
I'll—never mind—good afternoon.

Part Four

BIBLES & REFORM

RELIGION HAS ALWAYS PLAYED a key role in the carceral life. The word *penitentiary* itself is based on the religious concept of penance. And penance is predicated on sin. In the early nineteenth century the New York Prison Association, one of the earliest reform groups, took as its motto the phrase, "Sin no More." Incarceration was to induce a penitential frame of mind and lead to a reformation of character. Religion has indeed played a beneficial part in reforming or rehabilitating many convicts. The solitude and inner pressure to change one's life for the better often leads a person to seek spiritual solace, comfort, and help. Little wonder that so many convict memoirs focus on religion and the conversion experience. We could do a book in itself on the conversion narrative, but that would leave our impression of nineteenth-century prison life decidedly skewed. The selections presented here are representative examples of the felon who finds God in prison. They do not have the exhilarating spiritual fullness as the imprisoned John Bunyan, but they do express an unmistakable sincerity of religious devotion.

Henry O. Wills's narrative contains most of the elements that constitute a reformed criminal. He describes undergoing the tortures of the shower bath, the iron collar, working in the mines, and other punishments. But for him the *solitude* of the dungeon was the worst; the dungeon literally put the fear of God into him and he converted. Upon release from prison, he became an evangelist preacher. Following a life of crime, Franklin Carr found God after hearing about the Jerry McCauley Mission in New York City. This is the same Jerry McCauley who writes of his own transformation in Sing Sing when "the glory of the Lord shone in his cell." J. Wess Moore expresses his religion through poetry.

Many have found religion in prison, but Andrew George in *The Texas Convict* believed that "reform must start with the man himself" who is given opportunities to change his ways. George's view reflects in some respects the Progressive movement's aims of reformation through the improvement of the ex-offender's environment. We saw more of this type of literature as the twentieth century advanced and reformers probed for the causes of crime. The idea of rehabilitative programs for prisoners had taken root after the National Prison Congress in 1870, gathering steam for the next fifty years, and set the prison reform agenda for much of the twentieth century. Most reform programs failed. What remains constant in the convict literature of reform are two not necessarily mutually exclusive concepts: the reliance on the self as an autonomous moral agent and the transformative and redemptive power of religion.

The Great Turning Point of My Life

BY HENRY O. WILLS

From *Twice Born; Or, The Two Lives Of Henry O. Wills, Evangelist; Being a Narrative of Mr. Wills's Remarkable Experiences as a Wharf-Rat, a Sneak-Thief, a Convict, a Soldier, a Bounty-Jumper, a Fakir, a Fireman, a Ward-Heeler, and a Plug-Ugly. Also, a History of his Most Wondrous Conversion to God, and of his Famous Achievements as an Evangelist* (Cincinnati: Western Methodist Book Concern, 1890).

I was always at the caucuses and conventions, and to-day, as I sit and write this account, I believe the meanest of all devils, and worse than all thieves on earth, is the low "ward politician." He will steal the votes and stuff the ballot-box, and an honest man has no more chance in a caucus than the devil has of getting to heaven.

One of the greatest things I have to regret, among so many hundreds which I do regret, is that I was a Democratic howler and thief. I don't say, and I do not believe that all Democrats are thieves. Horace Greeley once said that all horse-thieves were Democrats, but all Democrats were not horse-thieves. I say that all Democrats are not as bad as I was. I never could see much difference between the Republican and the Democratic ward politician; but I honestly believe, from what I have seen, that the very, very little difference is in favor of the honesty of the Republican. I learned so much about both parties that I knew the victory would always be where the money was.

Now, before I tell about the great turning point in my life, which I spoke of, which was just after the fall caucus, October 5, 1883, where I had done my share of stealing votes, I wish to talk about some of the terrible things I have been through; things which I have suffered, because I was so wicked, and things which I have not yet spoken of.

I have been showered with ice-cold water, out of the mines; I have worn the ball and chain; I have been bucked, and I have worn the iron collar with a padlock to keep it on, and it needed no starch to keep it stiff.

O, what terrible punishments I have had! But I never squealed or hollered in my life but twice. Once in Clinton Prison, when I was locked up in the dungeon; and once in Detroit, which I will tell about when I write the story of the turning point in my life. This story will tell how God manifested himself to me.

I have often wondered that but one man in Detroit ever spoke to me about hell. This one man was W.H. Suite. He used to say to me, "Wills, you are surely going to hell if you keep on in the way you are going," and I would answer: "All right; I will have lots of company when I get there." And now, whenever I tell the wicked what God says, "The wicked shall be cast into hell, and all the nations that forget God" (Psa. ix, 17), some of them answer me as I did Suite—that they will have lots of company.

Now as to the time I was locked up in the dungeon in Clinton Prison. This dungeon was a hell. On each side of me was a cell, and both were occupied. Above me was another, while in front a guard passed every half hour. Still there was no company for me. No man can describe how awful it is. Imagine yourself in a bank-vault, with the door shut on you, and you aware of the fact that they had lost the combination, are certain that you will never get out. Do you think either the guard outside or those above and around you would be any company for you? O, how dark my dungeon was! So black and dark was it that it seemed thick with black space, and full of lifeless air. No company for me. If we continue in our wickedness, and do not repent of our sins, the darkness of a dungeon will be bright sunlight, compared to the terrible darkness of hell, where the wicked will surely go.

I used to think in those days that I had a little "sand," and could stand punishment, but it was nothing. We had a prisoner called Tom Kelly who was the devil in the flesh—like Christ was the Lord in the flesh. He was sent to Sing Sing from New York City for twenty years for burglary in the first degree, but he was transferred to Clinton Prison, because they could do nothing with him. He was always trying to escape, and, always failing, invariably got punished for the effort. After he was in the Clinton Prison a week or two, he resumed his schemes and working to escape, and kept right on getting punishment. They would shower this man until he was drowned, then bring him to. The reader can have no conception how terrible this punishment is. Hands and feet in stocks, neck and head in a trough filled with ice-cold water, and with a towel packed around your neck so that the water comes up around your mouth. Then the keeper begins to talk to you. He asks if you will behave, and the minute you speak he pulls the string, and you don't have a chance to catch your breath. The little breath you have is taken away by the rush of cold water, and it don't take long to drown you.

Now, when the man Kelly was served in this way, and was brought to all shaking and shivering, as though his teeth would rattle out of his head, they would ask him if he would behave himself. He would take a breath, and then spit in their faces. Next, they would buck and gag him. To do this, they would handcuff Kelly's wrists together tightly. Then they made him sit on the stone floor of the cell, with his heels drawn as closely to his buttocks as possible, thus forcing his knees close up to his breast. Then his fastened hands would be passed over his knees, an arm on either side of his legs. Next a short iron bar would be passed through, over the arms and under the knees, and there he was absolutely helpless. Next a wooden gag would be put in his mouth, and tightly fastened there by means of cords passing around either side, and tied at the back of the head. Thus restrained, and with no support except the floor, Kelly would sit upright as long as possible, and then, through pure fatigue, fall over to one side or the other, and lie there until some keeper would come along and set him up again. It is a hellish punishment, and becomes absolute torture in a very short while.

But Kelly was a man of iron will, and with the disposition of a bull-dog. Of course he could not speak while bucked and gagged, and when they would take out the gag that he might say whether or not he would behave, he would again spit in their faces.

The keeper would say: "Will nothing tame this man?" Then I heard some of them say: "Yes, yes; forty-eight hours in the dungeon will make even this devil crawl over the stone flags in the hall of the prison, and beg like a whipped school-boy. So into the dungeon he goes."

Let me tell how one feels while in this dungeon. It seems as though the walls were coming together, and that, closing in on you, you would soon be in a stone coffin, unable to move a finger. Then you get so hungry, it seems as though you could eat a stone, and there, right before you, would appear tables loaded with food, rivers of waters, and banks of fruit, and you not able to even touch a thing, or stoop to get a drink. Next the awful room would seem filled with all the devils in hell, who had come for you and were dancing all around you, grinning and shooting fire-balls at you. You need not shout, no one can hear you; the doors are too thick, and the walls are very heavily built of stone.

Well, this was the hell where Kelly was put, and when his time was up they asked him if he would behave himself, if they would let him out.

"O God, yes!" he cried in terror; "let me out! I will behave."

Thus, you see, may the horrors of a dungeon on earth, made by the hands of man, affect a strong man. What then must be the suffering of those to whom God will say on that great day, "Bind him and cast him into outer darkness," where there will be weeping and wailing! Compared to the sufferings in a dungeon made of stone, it will be as an ocean to a drop of water. When God locks the door of hell on us, the key or combination is lost forever. I pray that the words which are here written, by one whom God in his mercy has saved, may rescue some from this hell.

I used to say when in prison, when the minister was preaching (and he was a poor preacher, too): "I wonder if that man would be preaching like that, if, when a boy, he had been obliged to sleep in a fish-stand, or under the docks, or in a dry-goods box?" Then I would say: "I could be good, too, if some one paid me for it, as they paid him, at the rate of one thousand five hundred dollars a year. I, too, would be good if I had nothing to do but go around and talk, and read the Bible, and get paid for it."

Well, friends, the time did come when I, too, went around to preach and read the Bible, and I did not get the one thousand five hundred dollars either.

I hope no man will ever look to be converted just as I was. Just rest on God's promised word, and believe what he says. I have proved again and again that God spoke the truth when he said: "Be not deceived; God is not mocked: for whatsoever a man soweth, that shall he also reap." Hence I say, once again, don't wait to be converted just as I was, because you might not live to go through it. I happened to have "sand" enough to bear it, and you might not have this "sand." Don't wait, but believe in God now.

Cease to do evil, and begin to do well.

Now, as you read this book, is the time to begin. Take God at his word, and come to him just as you are; in prison or out of prison, God will receive you, because he has said: "He that cometh unto me I will in no wise cast out."

Real Reform

By ANDREW L. GEORGE

From *The Texas Convict: Sketches of the Penitentiary, Convict Farms and Railroads, Together with Poems* by Andrew L. George (N.P.: 1895).

It has been amply demonstrated in the history of crime that criminals can be reformed, at least some of them. My ideas about reform are short and simple—the reform must start with the man himself. It must be attended by a change of heart; he must desire to be a better man. He must be thrown into such surroundings that have a tendency to make him forget his old haunts of vice. Above all, he must be employed in some way. Most all who come out have some trade that they can work at. Now if there was some place where they had trades, such as chair making, carpeting, etc. Let there be a building superintended by some ex-convict. Then when a man from prison came here without money, let him be taken in, provided with food and lodging, and after paying for that at cost give him the balance. The goods manufactured thus could be sold and make the Convict Industrial Home self sustaining. Have bath, barber shops and library in connection. Another feature would be, we would have them under our eye and the chances of them committing crime would be diminished. Reforming is cheaper than punishment and we could no doubt bring some of them to believe that honesty is the best policy even viewed from the lowest motives.

Texas has an immense number of convicts, more than four thousand. Its crime keeps on increasing at the rate it has for the last two years we will be compelled to have six prisons instead of two.

Hence it is apparent that the convict question is a very important one and demands investigation and that prompt and active measures be taken for the enforcement of the criminal law, and the care, education and reformatory treatment of the convict after sending him there. This subject of reforming convicts at the present time is engaging the attention of our most thoughtful men. People who do not think, imagine when a convict is sentenced that's all, but what of the time when he is to come out, you never thought of that. He must be in a condition to be a better man when he comes out than when he went in. If he is just the same, he preys upon you again. The idea advanced by the Cottrell Protective and Detective association handles the subject in a masterly manner, and shows the reason why so many professional criminals escape conviction. His ideas are both for punishment and future protection. Under present conditions our prisons are only a mill for turning out criminals to prey on the community. Under the baneful influence of this political pest house, the morals of the country are being corrupted. It is a stench in the nostrils of all good and law-abiding people, and the sooner they stamp the life out of it the better for all concerned. It is a question that concerns every parent in the state of Texas. As it stands today, its corrupting and degrading influence may send your son in the prime of manhood and flush of talent to occupy the fittest earthly type of hell—a felon's cell. Your daughter, now pure and lovely as an angel, through it may be doomed to a life of shame in a den of infamy to decay in a potter's field, or dissected by a surgeon's knife—an unclaimed body from the morgue. O, thou God of my salvation! do not permit my friends or my loved ones to suffer such agonies in life and desecration in death. O, voice of genius! O, lips of eloquence! touched with a live coal from off the altar of human right and justice, assail it 'till truth, like hero armed in mail, shall strike to earth the hosts of tyrant wrong and hold eternal sway.

For myself I can say that this is the cock that will crow in the morn, when justice blows her delinquent horn, commanding the ring to step up and acknowledge the corn.

I reiterate everything I have said, both there and here in my public addresses and in these pages, and fling it back in their dastardly lying teeth. I have nothing but profound contempt for this whole gang of political criminals for their contemptible ignorance. The best of them have not as much education as a fifteen year old school boy. All they know is political crookedness. I now take my leave of them forever, hoping that they may, in the not remote future, cease to do evil and learn to do good; quit stealing from the state, but go to work and earn an honest dollar. You cannot always carry on such crookedness. "Murder will out." If you continue in this line of life, take my word for it, that sooner or later you will find that you have scattered thorns instead of roses for the gathering bye and bye.

Boys don't forget your mother is old
And weary with years that have passed;
Remember her care for you when you were young,
Her shelter of you from all evil blast.

Your mother has prayed for your welfare alone,
When God only heard what she said.
When in places where sin and evil are wrought,
Remember your mother instead.

Your mother has cared for you when you were sick
And turned the world to one side,
But the love of her is as strong as of old,
As the years of the world swiftly glide.

—Bardwell Waldo in Riverside

Outside

BY JERRY MCCAULEY

From *Transformed; or, The History of a River Thief, Briefly Told* by
Jerry McCauley (N.P.: Published by the Author, 1876).

> *"In the way a thousand snares*
> *Lie, to take us unawares;*
> *Satan, with malicious art,*
> *Watches each unguarded part."*

When I got out of prison I was as lonely as I had been in my
cell. I could not go back to my old haunts and companions, and
I knew no others. If I had found a single Christian friend it
would have saved me years of misery. And here I must say that
it does not seem to me right to turn men out of prison, and
make no provision for their future well-doing. Many a poor fellow has been driven to crime, and back again to his prison cell,
for want of kindly counsel and direction when he first came
out again into the world.

I wanted to do right, to please God. The first thing I did
was to inquire for a prayer meeting. I was told of one; but
when I got to the door I was afraid to enter. I had never been
to a Protestant place of worship, and nobody invited me in. I
kept steadily away from the Fourth ward, lest I should be
tempted by old associates. Most unfortunately the only friend
I found directed me to a lager-bier saloon to board. Lager-bier
had come up since I went to prison, and I did not know what it
was. They told me it was a harmless drink, wholesome and
good, and simple as root-beer. I drank, and that began my
downfall. My head got confused. The old appetite was awakened. From that time I drank it every day, and it was not long
before I went from that to stronger liquors.

The night I stopped praying I shall never forget I felt as
wretched as I did the day I went to prison. And now began a career of sin and misery which I cannot fully describe. Satan got
completely the upper hand of me. The dear Saviour who had

been so gracious and so precious to me in the prison I let go. How I wonder now that he did not let me go. But he did not.

I had obtained work in a large hat shop. The workmen had a strike, and I was one of the ringleaders. We were all dismissed and thus I was thrown out of employment. Then, it being war time, I went into the bounty business. Rascally business, that. I would pick men up wherever I could find them, get half drunk, and coax them to enlist. They received the bounty, and I had a premium on each of half the amount. I made a great deal of money in this way, which I spent freely. I became a sportsman, went often to the races, and my downward course was greatly quickened.

I got in with a man, who has since died of delirium tremens, and went boating on the river. We would buy stolen goods of the sailors, compel them to enlist on fear of being arrested, and we took the bounty. We went on for some time in this thieving, racing, speculating, and bounty business. We kept a recruiting office in New York, and another in Brooklyn, and found plenty to do, and might have grown rich if I had saved what I made.

But all this time my conscience was far from easy. I remembered the days at Sing Sing when the glory of the Lord shone in my cell, and I was shouting with joy for sins forgiven, and improving every moment to win souls to Christ. I knew I was all wrong, and yet I could not stop. I seemed to be on a down track, and rushing at furious speed. When I felt the most troubled I would go to drinking, and try to drown conscience in a glass of whiskey.

The Bright Side of Life
By Franklin Carr

From *Twenty-Two Years in State Prisons* by Franklin Carr (Philadelphia: Gazette Printing Co., 1893).

This young man, whom I met at the corner of Eighth and Vine streets, by the name of William H. Evans, was a Christian. He took me by the hand and said he was glad to see me, and asked me to go with him. He said his wife would be glad to see me, as she had not seen me for some time. I tried to put him off, saying I had to meet a couple of friends; but he insisted that I should go with him, saying that those kind of friends were never any good to me. At last I consented to go with him. After we had dinner and sat talking awhile, I said, "Well, good-bye, Willie; I will come and see you again." He asked me where I was going, and I told him I thought I would go up to Eighth and Vine a little while. He said he would take a walk up that way with me.

So we started out together, and he never lost sight of me until evening. Then he said I had better go and take supper with him, but I told him I would sooner go and take supper with my old friend, Mr. John A. Clayton, who had been more than a brother to me; he was my little playmate when I was six years of age, and who stuck to me when everybody else seemed to turn their backs on me. When I was in prison he would write to me and bring me anything that I was allowed to have, and I have lived with him ever since I have been out of prison. But Willie said I was too weak to walk down there for supper, and that I had better go and take supper with him.

After we had supper I bade him good-night, and he said, "Where are you going to-night?" I said I thought I would go to one of the theatres, so he said he would take a walk up that way with me. We walked about in the neighborhood of Eighth and Vine streets until we heard singing at a corner that used to be a saloon when I went to prison. It has since been converted into a mission. Willie Evans said to me: "Let us go in there awhile and hear them sing, and we can rest ourselves." We sat right in front of the superintendent, whose name was James Johnson, or, as they called him, Jimmy Johnson. He was telling how thieves and drunkards had been saved in the Jerry McAuley Mission in New York city, and I thought to myself, Can this be true that such bad men had been saved? It seemed to me that he was talking directly to me; and when they gave the invitation to raise the hand for the prayers of those good people, I looked around me and saw that those people had what I did not have, and I felt I would like to live a better life, if I could.

Willie told me to raise my hand, and I told him it was no use for me to do so. He told me it would do me no harm if it did no good, and then I raised my hand. It was not long before two or three of them got around me and told me that Jesus loved me; and I told them that they did not know how bad I had been. Then they told me it did not make any difference how bad I had been, and one lady invited me to go into the inquiry room. After a little hesitation, I got up and walked back in the room, and she talked to me and told me about Jesus and the story of the cross, and how He saved the thief in the last hour; and she told me what He did for the thief over eighteen hundred years ago He could do for the thief to-day. She said a good many other things about Jesus that I do not remember just now, but she told me to get on my knees and pray that Jesus would save me. I said I do not know how to pray, and then she said, "I will teach you how to pray." I stayed on my knees until nearly twelve o'clock that night, and then I went to the place where I was stopping and got on my knees again and stayed there until between two and three o'clock in the morning, when I felt as if a heavy burden had rolled off of me, and I felt like shouting for joy, for I knew that the Lord had heard my cry for mercy.

That was two years ago, and the Lord has taken care of me ever since. I have been going about from one church to another, and from one mission to another, telling what a wonderful Saviour I have found and speaking to those that were down in the gutter of sin and crime where I myself had been. I have known men to raise their hands for prayer just to get into the inquiry room to coax me out to take a drink, and they have even stood outside of the door and poked a bottle of whiskey under my nose to tempt me back into the world again, and I have had the detectives follow me around day after day and at last they arrested me for robbing a safe on Arch street that I did not know anything about, but God raised up good friends for me and brought me through all right, for I knew it would be easy to sentence me on my previous bad character and circumstantial evidence.

Since I have been preaching and telling others the story of the cross, the Lord has blessed me wonderfully.

I remain, your brother in Christ,

Franklin Carr
Philadelphia, Pennsylvania
January 5, 1893

Prayers

BY J. WESS MOORE

From *Echoes from the Tomb of the Living Dead* by J. Wess Moore, Life
Convict No. 18,759, California State Prison, San Quentin (Berkeley,
California: Keystone Publishing Co., 1908).

My Home Prayer

O Lord, forgive my evil deeds
*   In Thee I trust for all my needs*
No more I'll sow the cruel seeds,
*   For now, dear Lord, 'tis Thou who leads.*
I know my home in the valley old
*   Was a home of toil and love for gold*
Not so that home which did unfold
*   On Calvary's brow by Scripture told.*
O home, sweet home, O home of love,
*   May I ere long go home above*
And dwell with Him in peace and love
*   Within that home, sweet home above.*

The Penitent Convict's Prayer

Thou hearest, O God, in the morning,
*   Thou hearest at noon and at night,*
Thou hearest my prayer in the evening,
*   My sins lay bare to Thy sight;*
I mourn my awful condition,
*   While sorrows make heavy my heart,*
Because from the dear ones Thou gave me,
*   My sins hath set me apart.*
Father of love and great mercy,
*   I pray Thee while humbled I be,*
To grant my prayer of repentance,
*   My sins I bring all to Thee.*
My wrongs were cruel and many,
*   While Satan was leading along,*

Shame hath hidden my gladness,
    I live with the convict throng.
And now, dear Lord, I acknowledge,
    Although my confession is frail,
That Thou, in great love and mercy,
    Hath found me and saved me in jail.
Through the great, high walls of my prison,
    Thy Sun in my soul did shine
I received Thy love and forgiveness,
    So now, dear Lord, I am Thine.
O Father, forgive me for breaking
    The heart of a mother so dear,
And unite us again by Thy Spirit,
    And bring to her soul good cheer.
Dear Lord, forgive me for sowing
    The tares in the place of grain,
O Father please grant my petition
    There forever with Thee will I reign

ALSO FROM AKASHIC BOOKS

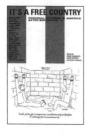

It's a Free Country:
Personal Freedom in America After September 11
Edited by Danny Goldberg, Victor Goldberg, and Robert Greenwald
370 pages, hardcover
$19.95, ISBN: 0-9719206-0-5
"A terrific collection of personal stories, legal arguments, and historical reminders about civil liberties in our society. We must never forget that we live in our faith and our many beliefs, but we also live under the law—and those legal rights must never be suspended or curtailed." —Reverend Jesse Jackson

R&B (Rhythm & Business):
The Political Economy of Black Music
Edited by Norman Kelley
338 pages, hardcover
$24.95, ISBN: 1-888451-26-2
"In this anthology, perhaps the first to deal solely with the business of black music . . . [t]he history of the modern recording industry . . . is dissected in several eyeopening contributions that should be required reading for anyone interested in popular music."
—*Library Journal*

We Owe You Nothing:
Punk Planet, the Collected Interviews
Edited by Daniel Sinker
334 pages, a trade paperback original (6" x 9")
$16.95, ISBN: 1-888451-14-9
"This collection of interviews reflects on of *Punk Planet's* most important qualities: Sinker's willingness to look beyond the small world of punk bands and labels and deal with larger issues. With interview subjects ranging from punk icons Thurston Moore and Ian MacKaye to Noam Chomsky and representatives of the Central Ohio Abortion Access Fund, as well as many other artists, musicians, and activists, this book is not solely for the tattooed, pierced teenage set. All of the interviews are probing and well thought out, the questions going deeper than most magazines would ever dare; and each has a succinct, informative introduction for readers who are unfamiliar with the subject. Required reading for all music fans." —*Library Journal*

DR. LARRY E. SULLIVAN is
Chief Librarian of the John
Jay College of Criminal
Justice and Professor of
Criminal Justice at the City
University of New York. He
is the author of *The Prison
Reform Movement: Forlorn
Hope* (Twayne, 1990), as well
as author or editor of numerous books and articles in
history, penology, and other
disciplines. Sullivan is cur-
rently the editor-in-chief of
the *Encyclopedia of Law Enforcement.*